To Eckhart Tolle, for helping me put the concept of ‘beyond’ into words.

Contents

PART ONE
EGO

PART TWO
PERSPECTIVE

PART THREE
ONENESS

PART FOUR
DEATH

PART FIVE
BALANCE

PART SIX
CHANGES

EGO

Walkden, Greater Manchester
September 2021

◇

Cristiano Ronaldo—Born to Be the Best

Endlessly Proving Oneself

At the end of the Northern English summer of 2021, as the days grew shorter, and the evenings began to feel cooler, a wind was blowing through the city of Manchester, bringing a sense of anticipation and excitement among the fans of Manchester United Football Club.

A few days earlier, the club announced that Cristiano Ronaldo had signed a new contract and now, at the age of thirty-six, would return to the city where his steep path towards glory commenced eighteen years ago.

David and Edo, two football-loving friends, originally from Eastern Europe, were enjoying a long passing session in Blackleach Country Park in Walkden, Salford. David was a lifelong, passionate Manchester United fan who had been living in Walkden for over ten years. Edo had arrived more recently and didn't support any club in particular but loved the game in general. Their different approaches to football represented a big difference in how they perceived the world.

"Nooo!" shouted David as he watched his friend soar heroically through the air attempting a bicycle kick before missing the ball entirely and hitting the ground in dramatic fashion.

"What are you doing, man?" David said in disbelief as he approached Edo, who was now stretched out across the luminous September grass holding his hip.

Edo flipped his skinny body onto his back with a look of shock in his eyes.

"Man?" said David.

"Shhh," Edo replied, requesting silence as his chest heaved laboriously. Finally, his face turned serene.

"That was crazy," David said, slumping his stocky frame beside Edo on the grass. "Are you alright, man?"

"Look how peaceful it is," Edo said, smiling, as the pair of them gazed up at the evening sky.

David's usual warrior-like, harsh face flashed with innocence as his lips stretched out in a smile. Even the great wrinkle between his eyes, which usually made him look angry, didn't seem as strained in the fading September sunlight.

"Did you just try to recreate Ronaldo's overhead kick against Juventus in Turin?" David said mockingly.

"I thought I had it for a moment," said Edo, still recovering. "It felt right to *go* for it."

"You were close," David said sarcastically.

They continued staring at the sky as the evening sun's rays bounced off their balding scalps.

"Ronaldo, though—" David remembered. "What a goal that was! It was the *perfect* bicycle kick—the composure—jump, kick, technique, style. Only the landing wasn't ten out of ten. But still, it was a *bit* better than yours."

Edo continued to gaze at the golden sun without even looking at David.

"—and then the epic celebration," David continued. "Running towards stunned and amazed Juventus fans while spinning his forefinger as if to say, *I am the one*."

"The *one*," Edo muttered under his still laboured breath.

"The number one," David repeated, sitting up quickly and pointing toward Old Trafford, the home of Manchester United, which seemed like a tiny red and white dot from where they were. "Ronaldo, *welcome home*!"

"Did you know Cristiano was an unwanted child?" Edo asked.

David turned to his friend in surprise.

"Unwanted?" he said. "What do you mean?"

Edo cleared his throat.

"Cristiano's mother, Dolores, wanted to have an abortion when she became pregnant with Cristiano. A doctor refused to do the operation, but Dolores was still determined to abort the baby, so she attempted to do it on her own. She admitted drinking boiled black beer and running until she felt like she would drop."[1]

"Wow, she said that?" David said. "That's one honest woman."

"*God's will* is what she calls it today," Edo continued. "—the fact she couldn't abort him."

David looked at Edo, who was still resting on his back, unmoving.

"Of course, it would have been a real shame if she had succeeded," David said. "Ronaldo is the greatest. His winning mentality is one of a kind. He always strives for more—to be better. *I was made to be the best*, he says."[2]

"What kind of person even says that?" Edo asked rhetorically. He finally turned his head to the right and looked at his friend with joyful, dark eyes which seemed to be completely absorbing the world and looking deeply into what he experienced. "I'll tell you what kind, David—someone who needs to prove something. A person who feels *rejected*."

"I believe such an attitude comes from pure hunger for success," David retorted.

"Well, I swear it all started in the womb," said Edo, leaning up onto one elbow.

"The womb?"

"Yes, in his mother's womb. The moment he experienced that scent of boiled black beer while enjoying his bath in amniotic fluid, he must have been like, *You want to get rid of me? I don't think so!*"

"God's will?" David said, questioning the words of Ronaldo's mother.

"You will see, mother," said Edo, dramatically playing the part of foetus Cristiano. *"I will be the greatest and make you the greatest mother of all. You will regret spilling beer all over me."*

"So rejection?" David said. "You're saying that all the answers to Ronaldo's greatness lie in rejection?"

"*All* the answers," Edo said, nodding. "Cristiano once said that winning was still his ultimate ambition, even after four hundred matches for Real Madrid. He believes he was born like that. He had the words *El sueño del niño* engraved on his boots—*The child's dream.*"[3]

"So from the moment he came to the earth, it was obvious," said David. "From the moment he first kicked a ball, it was clear. The *Cristiano Ronaldo mentality* was born?"

"It would seem so, David," Edo said, rubbing his itchy nose.

"But wouldn't that also mean that a failed abortion is entirely the basis of Cristiano's greatness?" David asked.

"Ego—" said Edo with a sigh.

"Ego?" said David screwing up the great wrinkle between his eyes in confusion.

"Yes," said Edo. "Cristiano's ego is based on *rejection*. It's a matter of life and death for him. It's about proving to himself and others that he is worthy. *Either he is the number one, or life is not worth living*. He needs to prove that his life was worth coming into existence."

"And he does prove it!" David said suddenly.

Edo nodded and continued.

"When Cristiano says that he hates losing, he's not just saying it for the cameras. He means it *one hundred per cent*. When he loses, he feels *genuine* misery and depression. If he deeply believes he was made to be the best, what happens when he doesn't deliver? If he sincerely believes he was born to be the best, then he has so much room to suffer."

"Yeah, only *one* can be the best," said David.

"Exactly," said Edo. "Do you remember the final match of *Euro 2004* in Portugal?"

"I do remember!" said David. "When Greece, against all odds, beat Portugal on their home ground and won the European Championship!"

"Yes," said Edo. "Then you must remember the tears of a then nineteen-year-old Ronaldo. Oh, he was so young and in such pain. He didn't want to exist at that point. How sad he was! I believe those were the most famous tears in footballing history."

"Yes, I remember," said David. "Fortunately, he hasn't lost many finals in his career. I believe he has only lost nine out of thirty-two finals. Some could have gone terribly for him, such as the 2008 Champions League Final in Moscow when he missed that penalty against Chelsea. Thankfully, John Terry slipped while taking the crucial penalty, and we got back in the series to eventually win it." David sat up, pulled his shirt, kissed the Manchester United badge on his chest and began singing, "*Glory, Glory, Man United!*"

"Right," Edo said, still lying down on the grass. "Ronaldo's teammates saved him, and eventually, he was awarded the Ballon d'Or for the best player in the world that year—his first one! He had fulfilled his ultimate victory—and he doesn't deserve to be rejected. He deserves to live."

"He *was born to be the best*," David said, echoing Ronaldo's words. "He is a god of football, any way you look at it. And he *knows* it."

"He does know it. He *knows* he is a god. He knows it!" Edo repeated ironically. "But David, don't forget, if being a god depends on being better than others, that means one more thing—Satan is dwelling there as well."

David lay back down again, taking a piece of grass and playing with it in his fingers.

"I don't see what Satan has to do with this," said the big man uncomfortably.

“*Ego*!” Edo exclaimed again, giving a gentle massage to his now-aching hip as if checking for damage.

“What about it?” said David.

“Well,” said Edo. “If Cristiano truly believes he is a god, that is the action of Satan—convincing him of something that inevitably imprisons him with the ego. Because ego restricts your soul—ego suffocates. Ego puts a tight rein on your freedom. Ego divides you from others. Ego makes you a god but for the price of Satan.”

“Go on, my friend,” said David, encouraging Edo to keep philosophising.

Edo nodded and continued.

“To carry the burden of God is not easy. Tell me, David, what happens when a man who believes he is a god must descend from his heavenly abode or, perhaps, when that same man learns there is another who comes from the land of Argentina and is considered by many as the *only* true football god?”

“Well, he is not happy, I guess,” said David.

“Correct, David,” said Edo. “He is *not* happy at all. He starts to prove himself. He shows off, convinces, agonises, and tortures himself while constantly stressing and explaining. And Satan? Well, Satan simply observes and enjoys the show. *Dance! Dance, oh God Almighty,* he says. *Now you're in my world.*”

“Wow,” said David, his mouth hanging open in the cool evening air.

“On the other hand,” Edo continued. “Do you know that type of man who is unchained from his ego?—the type of man who doesn't compare himself to others?—who is okay with who he is? *That* is a man who knits the net with God—who sings the song of *freedom*."

"But Edo," said David, placing a hand on his friend's back. "Surely, without such an ego, Cristiano Ronaldo would never have become the greatest. He would never have become the idea of success, and the mythological number seven he carries on his shirt would still be just another number. Nor would Manchester United be what it is. Ronaldo, bring the title *home* at last!"

The Game of Survival

Is There Space for Compassion?

"I think I've hurt myself," said Edo, checking on his hip again and finally standing up.

"I'd be surprised if you haven't," said David. "That effort was mental. I didn't see it coming at all. How bad is it?"

"Not great," Edo mumbled, controlling the ball skilfully with his right foot. "But it is what it is."

"I'm glad it wasn't me," David said in a concerned tone. "I couldn't afford to be injured. I need to work. My bakery can't run itself. Now lockdown is finally over, maybe I could earn enough for a good car—maybe even one of those from Ronaldo's garage. He has more than twenty cars in his garage, though. I would be fine with just one!"

"Cristiano has more than twenty cars in his garage?" said Edo. "Wow! I mean—houses, cars, ladies—it's like a constant need to show off. It's a special sort of ego that some football players have—me, myself and I. But—" Edo paused and looked at his friend. "Can we really blame them, David?"

"Right!" David said. "They have put *so much* into the game—effort, sacrifice, passion—they *deserve* everything—especially Ronaldo!"

Edo shook his head.

"No, David. That is not the reason we can't blame them. In my opinion, none of that is a justification for ego."

"Why can't we blame them, then?" said David.

"Pass me the ball," said Edo.

"Why can't we blame them?" repeated David as he rolled the ball to Edo, who didn't seem too concerned with his hip anymore.

"Well, let's put it this way," said Edo, receiving the ball on his right instep. "Football is the *only* profession in the world where you can't be happy if you don't make somebody else sad."

"What do you mean?" said David, beckoning for the ball back.

Edo passed him the ball.

"Well, exactly like that," he said. "All of your success is based on the suffering of your opponent. Try to realise how bad that sounds. In football, your win and subsequent happiness inevitably include someone else's loss and sadness."

David nodded his understanding.

"No compassion there!" Edo declared. "You simply can't be a footballer *and* have a high degree of compassion. The laws of football don't allow for that."

"Are we talking about ego or compassion here?" asked David.

"Well, they are connected," said Edo, signalling for the ball again. "Low compassion means big ego—and vice versa. High compassion means small ego. Compassion encompasses care for others, but football laws don't let you care for others because that would mean allowing others to win. Therefore, if there is no care for others, there is only care for yourself—ego!"

David side-footed the ball to his friend and Edo played it back too quickly, missing his target and shooting it miles past David.

"Sorry, man," said Edo as he watched David jog after the ball.

"So high ego means low compassion, then?" David shouted back before finally reaching the ball and jogging back with it at his feet.

"Yes!" Edo shouted back. "And the bigger the stakes, the more the lack of compassion is expressed. Just try to recall the scenes after Edwin van der Sar saved Anelka's penalty to win the Champions League for United on that rainy night in Moscow."

David clenched his fists with excitement.

"I can see it now!" he said. "The guys are racing towards the goalie in complete delirium, trying to get their heads around what's happening. Ronaldo is reprieved, lying face down in the grass, his whole body shaking. Van der Sar is going through a metamorphosis, howling like a wolf on his knees. He is in a trance as Carrick and Fletcher lift him up. Sir Alex Ferguson comes onto the pitch, arms wide open, hugging his players. They are all happier than they'd ever been. They are over the moon. *We* are over the moon! The players have reached the peak of their lives. The world was *ours* that night!"

"Exactly, David," said Edo. "And now try to remember the scenes in the losing team."

"Remind me," said David.

Edo nodded somberly.

"I *will* remind you, David." He took a deep breath. "Nicolas Anelka, who had just *profoundly* betrayed his teammates and fans by missing the penalty, was holding his head in sheer disbelief. Ballack was in tears. Frank Lampard—Mr Chelsea—was gutted and walking around the pitch, trying to catch his breath. And John Terry—the team captain—the man who slipped while taking the decisive penalty was sobbing, desolate, covering his face with his shirt. It was the worst day of his life. The entire team was utterly devastated."

"Yes! I do remember Terry looking completely soulless," David confirmed.

"Indeed!" said Edo. "And that means one thing only—that Edwin van de Sar did his job right. He made that night at the Luzhniki Stadium the worst night of John Terry's life. Manchester United did their job right. They made that night the worst night for the Chelsea players. And *that's* why I said earlier that you can't blame footballers for being egoistic beings."

"I see—" David said dubiously. "Laws of the game then, Edo?"

"Yup!" Edo said, juggling the ball with a sorrowful hip.

David scratched his head.

"Prove me wrong, my friend, but isn't that the law of every profession?"

"What do you mean?" said Edo.

David took a step closer.

"You said that football is the only profession where you have to make your opponent sad for you to be happy," he said.

Edo nodded.

"But that goes for every other profession as well," David continued. "Take for instance, my bakery here in Walkden."

"I do like the garlic bread you make," Edo said, dropping the ball and giving himself another small hip massage with his fist.

"Thank you," said David, bowing to his friend. "However, as you know, there is another bakery two blocks down, owned by Arafat. What I'm trying to say is, I feel happy when a customer enters my bakery, not Arafat's, even though that makes Arafat sad. I guess that's my hospitality ego. But in the end, it's about surviving. Ego is about survival, isn't it, Edo?"

"Yes, David, but—"

"Oh, fuck, Edo. I just realised—football is life," David said, interrupting his friend. "It's just a magnified form of it, but the laws are essentially the same."

"Unless—" Edo began.

"Shit!" David said, stunned by his own conclusion. "If the law of life is to compete and survive, then you can't blame *any* football player for having a big ego. Indeed, it is a matter of evolution. Ego wins games. Ego makes money. Football is a game of egos."

"A time has come when we might need to change the course of evolution in order to survive as a species," Edo finally managed to say. "Because the current survival mindset—the current egoic patterns might take us to extinction."

"How can we change something so deeply rooted in what we are, though?" said David.

"Well," said Edo. "Let's not forget that a few times throughout football history, we have witnessed some true acts of compassion regardless of the final score. For instance, Kahn and Cañizares! Remember the Champions League final in 2001 between Bayern and Valencia at San Siro? It was a game of penalties where both goals were scored from the spot before the game went into a penalty shootout, and Bayern claimed the victory after Oliver Kahn saved three kicks."

"Okay, so where is the compassion?" said David.

"I'm getting to it," said Edo. "After the penalty shootout, Kahn stopped celebrating the biggest achievement of his life to help a man on the losing side. He consoled his counterpart Santiago Cañizares who was utterly devastated and on his knees by patting him with his glove. When the final result created a distinction between winners and losers, Kahn stepped up and made them equal again, regardless of the result—that's what compassion is, David. I believe a simple touch of a glove helped Cañizares to feel better at that point."

"Glove understands glove," said David, bowing his head in respect for Kahn's action.

"Still, David, it was very different in 2014 when Real Madrid beat Atlético Madrid in the Lisbon final," Edo said. "It was one of the toughest games Atlético had ever played. Diego Simeone's players fought and sacrificed like brave lions for the whole season. Then, one week before this game, they had claimed the Spanish title for the first time in eighteen years. Now, facing Real Madrid, they were almost there after ninety minutes—at the roof of Europe. However, in the fourth minute of injury time, Luka Modrić's corner found Sergio Ramos, who headed it in to make it 1-1 and send the game into extra time.

The *Atlético* players were devastated. They were utterly exhausted and couldn't run anymore, having given everything.

Real ran them over, toying with the lapsed warriors. Gareth Bale scored for Real first before Marcelo claimed the victory a few minutes later. It was all over. Atlético players were barely standing on their feet. They wanted the final whistle to wrap their season, but—"

"But Ronaldo had something to say as well!" David said.

"Exactly," Edo continued. "In the last minute of the game, he was awarded a penalty. And he made sure he would take all the headlines for himself by scoring the penalty and running towards the crowd, taking his top off, flexing his muscles and celebrating as if he had scored the crucial goal of the game. He showed no compassion for the wounded opponent whatsoever. Only me, myself, and I. *I am the one!*"

David looked at his friend, nodding.

"Ronaldo survived!" he said with a grin.

Penalties—Me Versus Myself

A Mirror of the Mental State

"You can't deny Ronaldo's determination and will," David said. "And the mental strength that comes along with that."

"Elaborate, please," said Edo as the pair began to stroll aimlessly on the field, David kicking the ball ahead of him.

"Well—penalties, for instance," said David.

"I see where this is going," said Edo, picking the ball up and bouncing it every few steps.

"Penalties mirror a player's mental state," said David. "And Ronaldo is one of the best penalty-takers in the game's history, if not *the* best. To be a decent penalty taker, you must be mentally strong, my friend. Because when you place the ball on that eleven-metre mark, you become an executioner. The judge has convicted an offender for violating the rules, and you are assigned to do the rest—to carry out the execution."

"That's a bit harsh, David," said Edo with a smile.

His big friend nodded his agreement with wide eyes.

"It is," said David. "It's harsh as fuck, man. Penalties *are* harsh. It's pure survival!"

"It's true," said Edo. "Especially when it comes to penalty shootouts. Suffering is guaranteed!"

"Yes, penalties are not for the weak," said David, dumping his backpack on the ground. "Now, come on, Edo, my friend. Don't be a coward. Put your backpack down as the other goalpost, okay?" He took a few steps and pointed to a spot with his big arm. "Just about here should do."

Edo placed his backpack where David suggested while David picked up the ball and began taking steps from the newly created goal towards a suitable penalty spot.

"Now, recall the movie *The Green Mile,*" David shouted back at his friend who was standing between the backpacks. "It's about prisoners on death row waiting for their electric chair execution."

"Yeah, with John Coffey. It makes me cry every time," Edo said.

"Yes," said David. "So you must remember the executioners in the film then. Tom Hanks was one, and David Morse was the other."

"That's right," Edo said, rubbing his hip slightly and doing a couple of warm-up squats.

David took a few steps back from the ball and scratched his thick beard. "The role of those executioners was to pull the lever down and send the current straight to the offender's brain," he said. "Those guys were tough—*very* tough. They were very stable, as well, though. They had to be very down-to-earth, fairly routine kind of guys. But they were also cold-blooded, possibly even emotionless, when it came to the job they had to do. That is pretty much the psychological profile of a good executioner."

"So you are saying the best penalty takers also have that psychological profile?" said Edo, squatting slightly, hands on his knees.

David jogged up to the ball as if about to shoot. Edo braced himself, but David just picked up the ball with a smile.

"Yes!" he said. "Let me remind you of some of the greatest executioners—erm, sorry, I mean penalty takers beside Cristiano Ronaldo." David began waving his finger around as if pointing to an imaginary list. "Let's see now. There's Frank Lampard, Steven Gerrard, Zinedine Zidane, Alessandro Del Piero." He paused for a moment and replaced the ball on the same spot before continuing. "Harry Kane, Jamie Vardy, Sergio Ramos and Zlatan Ibrahimović are some recent examples."

"Nicely listed!" Edo said. He frowned at his friend in a friendly way. "You are too close to the goal, though. Go back a bit."

"All of them were strong-headed men," said David, shaking his head and picking up the ball again.

"Luck, they say," Edo said ironically.

"What luck?" David almost shouted as he replaced the ball another metre or so back.

"They say penalties are like roulette—based on luck," said Edo, nodding his agreement at the new ball placement.

David shook his big head again.

"Yeah, they say it because they don't get it, my friend. There is zero luck when it comes to penalties. If you are mentally strong enough, you only see the goal and the spot where the ball will burst the net. Ask Jamie Vardy if you don't believe me," David said and scrunched up the big wrinkle between his eyebrows, which gave him an overly severe look.

"Ah yes, David," said Edo in an animated way. "But you are forgetting that there is also a *goalkeeper* to be asked something."

"Not, really," said David. "A good taker won't even see the goalie." The big man put his chin on his chest, took a deep breath and looked at the ball. He lowered his tone. "That's what mental strength is, Edo. The goalie doesn't stand a chance if you can hit the spot you imagine. You are shooting against yourself. It's just you and a keeper strapped in an electric chair waiting to receive two thousand volts. All you need to do is calmly pull that lever."

Edo retook his stance, legs slightly apart and hands on knees.

"You look nervous!" he said, teasing David who lined up to take the shot.

"It was 2018," David said calmly as he lengthened his spine. He lifted his head again to look Edo in the eyes. "Real Madrid were playing Juventus in the second leg of the quarter-finals at Santiago Bernabéu. A week earlier, Real Madrid, on the wings of Ronaldo's bicycle kick, won 3-0 in the first leg in Turin, and now after climactic ninety minutes, Juventus have made a dramatic comeback to lead 3-0 and take the game into extra time—drama at its finest. However, in the ninety-seventh minute, Benatia tackles Vázquez, and the referee Michael Oliver awards Real a penalty. Desperate Juventus players are running towards Oliver. The great Gianluigi Buffon is threatening him and gets a red card. Real players are joining the brawl. The fans are delirious. Wojciech Szczęsny is getting ready to replace Buffon between the goalposts. It's utter chaos, my friend."

"Sounds like it," said Edo, standing up straight yet again.

"Do you know who isn't joining the brawl?" said David.

"I think I can guess," said Edo. "Cristiano Ronaldo?"

"Correct, my friend," David said. "Ronaldo is standing far away from the chaos with the ball in his hands. He doesn't even see the fight. He doesn't see Buffon getting the red card. He doesn't even notice somebody is replacing Buffon in goal. Ronaldo doesn't hear the deafening sound of eighty thousand hysterical fans. He only sees the ball and himself. He places the ball on the white spot, takes one last look at the ball, and then one more time into himself—first, the deep breath, then the shot. The ball flies into the top right corner. Szczęsny dives in the right direction, but he is nowhere near the ball."

"So Cristiano knew what he was doing," said Edo.

David nodded.

"Just Cristiano Ronaldo—a keeper in the electric chair—and the lever slowly pulling down. Two thousand volts straight to the offender's head—zzappp," David said, imitating the motion of pulling down the lever with his right hand.

"That would have been crazy," said Edo, imagining the scenes from Santiago Bernabéu.

"Crazy," said David. "And Ronaldo's strong ego also plays an important role here, Edo. His *I am the best* ego gives him an edge—extra mental strength when playing the executioner. It gives him that extra determination to survive and kill the enemy."

"Correct," said Edo. "For when there is execution, there is ego. But inevitably, there is also suffering—for *everybody* involved, one way or another. The mental strength that rests on *I am the best* must have a flip side, just as everything that rests on such a mindset has its flip side."

"What I want to say, Edo," said David. "Is that when you are as mentally strong as Ronaldo or, perhaps, Harry Kane, you just need to pull the lever. But what happens when a penalty taker is not as mentally strong? In *The Green Mile*, apart from Tom Hanks and David Morse, there was another executioner, played by Doug Hutchison. If I remember correctly, Percy was the character's name—a small, sadistic guy."

"Yeah, the guy who killed the mouse," Edo said, now squatting and playing with a piece of grass. "He pissed his pants just as you are pissing yours now."

David smiled at his friend.

"He wasn't a stable person." David continued. "He didn't have what it took to be an executioner. He was mentally weak. Therefore, he was not able to execute properly for whatever reason. There's a scene in the film when he doesn't soak the sponge in water when he puts it on the offender's head."

"I remember," Edo said. "So he put a dry sponge on his head before sending the electricity through the sponge, and the poor guy burns to death after minutes of inexplicable agony."

"Yeah, that's the one."

"That guy was completely insane," Edo said, standing up and assuming his stance again. He pointed to the left side of the goal. "Come on, let's go. Shoot it already," he yelled, making a face like a lunatic.

"You don't have to tell me twice," said David. He straightened his spine, took a deep breath and smashed the ball into the right corner beside the backpack.

Edo fell on his back, laughing and smiling at the sky.

"You pulled the lever, and now I'm dead," he said.

Protecting the Identity

Image Based on Thoughts and Emotions

"You see, my friend, life is about survival of the fittest," David said, stretching out his massive arm and pulling Edo to his feet. "Ego is about survival. I am a survivor. Ronaldo is a survivor!"

"Yes," Edo said, scowling as he squatted to test his hip. "But since there is no real danger to Cristiano's life while playing football, we must ask ourselves what kind of survival his ego is interested in? What is he trying to protect? What is his ego really about—in its essence?"

"What *is* ego in its essence?" David repeated, curiously.

The pair picked up their backpacks and strolled after the ball which had landed at the other side of the field due to the strength of David's shot.

"The way I see it, ego is essentially identification with something," said Edo.

"Something?"

"*Whatever*," Edo exclaimed. "Whatever you identify with becomes part of ego—of identity. Put it this way—do you support any club in particular?"

"Seriously?" David said, putting his chin on his chest and looking at his red shirt. "You know I support Man United."

"Of course," said Edo. "But what does that support imply?"

David raised his eyebrows and thought about it for a moment.

"Well, I love the club. I attend our games when I have a chance and I chant loudly," he said. "When we lose, I'm sad, when we win I'm happy. I'm loyal. It makes me part of something bigger—a part of a community."

"You see, that is ego *right there,*" said Edo, stopping suddenly and facing his friend. "The moment you *identify* with Manchester United, the club becomes part of your *identity.* And how do you *know* if the process of identification happened? Well, you just said it, David—*our* games. You meant it. You see Manchester United games as *your* games."

"I sure do!" said David, lifting his shirt again and kissing the badge.

Edo turned and started strolling again before continuing to speak.

"English fans go as far as saying, *I am* Manchester United, *I am* Arsenal, or *I am* Liverpool when asked what club they support," he said. "That's how strong identification with clubs in England is."

"It's called passion, my friend. It's called love for the club," David said. "I wear the Manchester United badge proudly on my chest, and I'm here to defend the colours of my club—always."

"To *defend* your club?" Edo repeated suspiciously. "You see—whenever there is identification with something, there are inevitably enemies there as well, and a notion of defending something. Fans who fully identify with the club's badge become soldiers of their clubs with a mission to conquer other armies—other clubs. Subsequently, you don't see the picture clearly anymore, but only through subjective perceptions. The club's defeats become a bad thing for you, while its wins become a good thing for you. Liverpool becomes your enemy and Manchester United players your idols. Of course, it's entirely the opposite for Liverpool fans. Once you identify with the club's colour, compassion is gone. *You* identify with Manchester United—compassion is gone."

"Of course," said David. "Life, growth, evolution. The *law* of the game—*survival*!"

"Well, yes," said Edo. "But what is survival really about here, David? It's not your *life* that is in danger. So what are you really defending? You are defending that image—the identity that *you* have created."

"What identity?" said David.

"Your *I'm Man United* identity," said Edo. "You want to preserve that identity because it gives you *meaning*. You seek meaning through the physical form."

"Seek meaning through physical form?" David said, confused and setting off into a light jog.

"Yes," said Edo, raising his voice and reluctantly jogging after David. "Identifying with physical form in an attempt to reach the completion—*meaning*. But ironically, lasting meaning can never be found through physical form—only temporary meaning. Let me ask you something very profound, David," said Edo, stopping his friend with a hand on his chest. "Does the identification with Manchester United make you *better*? Does it make you more of a human being? Does it make you better than a person who identifies as Liverpool? What does a Liverpool fan's identification with Liverpool make him? Are you more complete than him essentially? Or are those simply ego-created labels? Do you get what I am talking about, David? What does it mean that *he* is Liverpool and that *you* are Manchester United?"

David was not satisfied. He put a hand on his friends shoulder and they continued walking.

"All the suffering in the world comes from such identification, from ego," said Edo.

"Yeah," said David. "But in that case, also all the excitement and all else that life is worth living for. I will never forget the feeling when we won the Champions League in Moscow. It was one of the best days of my life! What a joy! What a rollercoaster of emotions! The moment Anelka's penalty was saved, we were all one big happy family. Ronaldo's tears of joy were *our* tears as well," David said and fell to the ground clenching his fists together as if reliving the victory.

Edo stopped and looked down at the big man, splayed out on the grass.

"That's interesting," he said. "Because Cristiano never had such a strong identification with any of the clubs he played for. He never felt such loyalty to Manchester United as you do, David. It was certainly never the *I am Manchester United* identity he was protecting. That's not what *Cristiano's* battles for survival were about."

"Maybe this time, his second time at the club, he really becomes Manchester United to the fullest! We believe in him!" said David, closing his eyes with hope.

"I doubt it," said Edo. "Cristiano's identity is not derived from *physical* form—at least not to the highest extent. Cristiano protects his self-created identity—*I am the best in the world*. Just as one can seek meaning through the physical form and the club's badge, one can seek it through the image created by thoughts and emotions. When you identify with your thoughts, they become part of your identity. That's *always* an unconscious process."

David looked confused again.

"Okay," said Edo. "That's the case with Cristiano. He's very identified with the thought, *I need to be the best*. And where does that thought come from, David? We established that earlier. It comes, perhaps, from his childhood trauma—from *rejection*."

"Rejection," David repeated vaguely.

"When Cristiano loses a match," Edo continued. "That situation is contrary to the egoic image of *the best in the world* he has created, so subsequently the thought of *not being good enough* makes him very anxious and feeds his trauma. Then the trauma once again generates the thought *I need to be the best*. It's a never-ending cycle of chasing the meaning—happiness."

"Well—That's what differentiates the best players from the rest of them," David said as he finally reached the ball, flicking it up with his toes and catching it. "—the fact they're never *satisfied*."

"True," said Edo. "But what happens when that thought isn't grounded in reality? It's the very thought that made Cristiano suffer from 2009 until 2012. That must have been the most difficult period of his career!"

"Why? What about that period?" said David.

"Lionel Messi!" Edo exclaimed like a prophet, lifting his arms in the air, imitating Messi's goal celebration. "Leo Messi was awarded the best player in the world on four consecutive occasions. Cristiano must have been devastated."

"He *must* have been," David agreed. "But then, because of that thought, *I need to be the best* and his determination to live up to it, he eventually won the award again in 2013."

"Correct," said Edo. "When Pelé announced his name at the Ballon d'Or ceremony, Cristiano was rescued from his agony. He bent his head briefly and breathed new life into his meaning. Then he stood up and burst into tears. That was the most emotional moment of his life—becoming the best once again after four long years of suffering."

"Yes!" David said victoriously.

"Identification with physical form, emotions and thoughts fuel actions and the search for meaning," Edo continued. "Ultimately, Cristiano has created an immense egoic structure—the brand CR7. That brand symbolises his absolute desire to be the best. *That* is what he defends. *That* is what his survival is about. Cristiano would die for that, just as *you—David—*would die for Manchester United. But as soon as Cristiano can't live up to that standard anymore, he will suffer, mark my words. The ego keeps him perpetually unsatisfied and separates him from the truth."

"And what is the truth?" said David, bouncing the ball and strolling off again.

"I'm glad you asked, David," said Edo with a smile. "Just as you are not essentially Manchester United, Cristiano is not essentially *his trauma.* Nor is he essentially the brand *CR7*. Those are all simply labels you embody when you unconsciously identify with them. So, at some level, you might be all of that, but only on the surface. Your labels are not essentially *you,* David. And Cristiano's labels are not essentially him."

David strolled beside his friend, taking it all in as the air temperature dropped.

"So what *is* Ronaldo essentially?" David asked, stopping to put on his tracksuit.

Edo also took his tracksuit out and began to put it on.

"He is essentially already complete," Edo said. "That's the truth. Beneath all those layers of ego, Cristiano Ronaldo is whole. Just as you are, David. Just as *we all are*."

"OK—" said David, the big crease between his eyes dipping into confusion.

Edo sensed his friend's confusion. "Ego is any identification that causes you to mistake your true identity with form," he said.

"What is Ronaldo's true identity then?" David asked.

"Something way bigger!" said Edo, waving his arms like a fisherman telling a tall tale.

"Bigger than *CR7*?" David said, his confusion growing even more. "Are you *sure* about that?"

Edo smiled, kicked the ball ahead, and they both chased after it.

Lesson by Lesson

The Core Rule of Growth

The evening sun dipped even further into the horizon, causing gold streaks to blaze across the sky. Still, the pair, now wrapped in tracksuits, were reluctant to leave the field despite the temperature drop.

"So you are saying that ego is essentially identification with something," David said as he sat down next to Edo, squeezing his knees with his arms to stay warm. "Well, ego wins games which only means that identification is crucial for winning. As we have established, your life is *not* at stake in football. So if you are not desperate to win to protect your life, you need to succeed in the name of something else—whether that is in the name of *I am Manchester United*, or *I am CR7*. Cristiano Ronaldo must have a deep sense of identification, otherwise, he couldn't have reached the heights he has."

"Yes, but—"

"No buts!" said David sharply. "What are you suggesting? That Ronaldo should not aim to win games, but perhaps, he should be content with drawing games?"

"Well, there's something very metaphysical about the draw, David," said Edo. He now had the look of a mystic. "The game is only liberated from misery when the match ends in a draw. There is no winning euphoria, but there is no suffering, either. A peaceful outcome appears in the balance between euphoria and misery."

"But football is not a game of peace," David objected. "It is a game of euphoria and suffering."

"Why couldn't it be a game of peace?" said Edo, turning to his friend. "Why are people so *afraid* of peace? Why can't we all live equally and be happy with what we have and with each other?"

A flock of geese flew over them, honking at the dying sun. Edo looked up at them peacefully. "Why can't football be a game of balance?" he said.

"Because there is no improvement in balance, no progress," David shouted, standing up. "Progress *requires* euphoria and misery, winning and losing. There is no *evolution* in balance, Edo."

Edo opened his eyes wide, struck by the argument.

"Yeah, about that," he said. "You need to be more specific, David. There might not be evolution in how *modern society* sees it—in how the modern mind *understands* evolution. But with peace, evolution would take *another* form."

"There would certainly not be evolution in the way society evolves—in the way football evolves," David said. The big man seemed to be getting a little irritated. "Take, for example, my bakery. If there was a balance, *half* of the customers would buy bread at my place, and the other half would buy bread at Arafat's bakery. Would I be at peace with that? Would Arafat be at peace with that?"

Edo waited for the answer, while David thought about it for a moment.

"Yes," David said, nodding gracefully. "There probably *would* be *peace*. But there wouldn't be *progress*."

"Again, what progress, man?" said Edo.

"Well, the progress of my bakery, for starters," David said, bending down to touch his toes before rubbing his cold thighs. "Let's say Arafat and I both produce sourdough bread, which we make in the same type of oven and we even price it the same. In theory, we share the customers because they don't care which bakery they buy bread in. Yes, there would be peace in the street, but that's *all* there would be."

"Sounds good to me!" said Edo, taking out a water bottle and drinking some before offering it to David.

David shook his massive head.

"On the other hand," David said while stretching his calves. "Evolution and growth *require* me to raise the stakes and produce double the sourdough bread that Arafat does. Progress *requires* me to buy a new oven that can produce Shepherd's loaf instead of sourdough loaf. Progress *requires* me to open a new bakery and take *all* the customers. If I took the majority of the customers, there would be potential for the growth of my bakery. I could extend the bakery or even build a new one down the street. I would be happy, and Arafat would be sad."

"The peace would be gone," Edo said.

"Yeah, but the growth is inevitable," said David. "Say, I have *three* new bakeries now, and I am producing Shepherd's loaves in my new, amazing electric dome ovens."

"But do you need three—"

"And *that's* what football is," David interrupted, punching the ball with his fist as he made the point. "You can't keep improving by *drawing* matches. You need to beat your opponents and make them sad for you to be happy. Winning is happiness, my friend. Losing is sadness."

They sat silently in the cool air for a moment.

"However!" David said, leaning into Edo with great importance. "However! There is also something valuable for Arafat—something precious indeed."

"And what is that?" said Edo.

"A lesson," said David.

"A lesson?"

"Every defeat brings a lesson," David said, standing tall. "Every loss makes you *stronger*."

Edo nodded. "That's very true, David," he said.

David looked excited at having made his point with Edo. "So do we agree that Arafat's loss of business would make him stronger as a person and not weaker?" he said.

Edo scratched his head for a moment before answering.

"Only if he recognises the learning process in losing and falling, I guess."

"Let me tell you something," said David, standing dominant over his friend. "Think of Manchester United from the era of Sir Alex Ferguson. That was arguably one of the most dominant dynasties in the history of football. Thirteen Premier League titles are clear proof! We played like no other team in the world!"

"That was a team like no other," Edo agreed. "The football they played—remarkable!"

"Then I guess you will remember what happened at the beginning of Ferguson's era," said David.

"Remind me," said Edo with a grin.

"Oh. *You* know it," David said, laughing.

"*Many* things happened," said Edo. "I would appreciate some help."

David took a long breath and held the ball tight with both hands, leaning into Edo again.

"Well," he began. "United were not doing well under Ferguson back then. Ferguson waited *seven* years for his first Premier League title."

"Seven years?" Edo said in surprise.

"*Seven* years!" David nodded. "Seven years of striving to survive as a manager—of striving not to get sacked. Seven years of *losing*. Can you imagine, Edo? Ferguson only won the first Premier League title in 1993, after he joined the club in 1986."

"Right," said Edo.

David crouched and rolled the ball from hand to hand.

"But Ferguson knew it!" he said. "He knew that every loss was a *lesson* to learn to get to the top. Every single loss was another brick towards building the empire." David made a circle with his hands now, pointing to Old Trafford in the distance. "Ferguson said later on, and I quote, *You have to treat losing as part of the progress. Throughout my life, I learnt failures spark something inside you. There is something about it. As a human being, you must understand adversity is part of life. And when it happens, define yourself.*"[4]

"That's wise," Edo said, nodding genuinely.

"After that, he won thirteen titles in the next twenty years," David said. "No doubt, every defeat was one step towards that perfection. Before he retired as a manager, Manchester United embodied football in its best form. Manchester United were a system with no faults. It was a *perfect* system."

"What a team!" yelled Edo, rolling playfully onto his back. "*The Class of 92!* The most illustrious group of graduates in the history of English football. *David Beckham, Paul Scholes, Ryan Giggs, Nicky Butt, The Neville brothers*—Ferguson realised the power of the academy and youth."

"That was the base," David said, nodding proudly. "But it couldn't have become a perfect system without hundreds and hundreds of defeats—without hundreds of times falling and getting up—without hundreds of lessons!"

"Ferguson recognised the learning process," said Edo, his eyes widening. "When one recognises it *for* what it is, then there are *no* defeats anymore. You *never* lose. You either win or learn."

David nodded, smiling at his friend.

"Then you can create a perfect system," he said.

Edo's forehead creased at the word *perfect.*

"The *perfect* system?" he said. "I'm not sure there is such a thing as perfection, David."

"Why not?"

Now Edo stood up and rubbed his hands on his thighs to keep warm.

"You can't claim that Manchester United from the end of Ferguson's era were a perfect system when the team was still losing games," he said.

"Right," said David in agreement. "To become a *perfect* system, you would, perhaps, need *all* the lessons in the world and all the *time* in the world. However, time limits us, so there *is* no such thing as perfection."

Edo winked at his friend and looked at the now dark blue sky.

"Only the universe as a whole is a perfect system," Edo said. "Only football as a whole is a perfect system. Jürgen Klopp said on one occasion that there is no perfect football team in the world because the game doesn't give you a chance to be perfect. If you can concede goals, you can lose."[5]

"Well, his club is *nowhere* near perfect," David said scornfully toward Liverpool FC. "Conversely, would it be fair to say that Sir Alex's Manchester United was as close to perfection as any club could get?"

Edo shook his head.

"United still lost against Barcelona in the two Champions League finals," he said. "In 2011, Barcelona were the strongest team in the world, so they demolished United."

"Yeah," said David. "Those were *two perfect systems* against each other."

Edo took up his usual dramatic stance.

"But the 2009 final was particularly epic with Pep Guardiola yet to become the *great* Guardiola," Edo said. "United arrived in Rome as a team who had beaten Arsenal so dominantly in the semi-finals, while Barcelona barely scraped into the final with the help of the referee Tom Henning Øvrebø who didn't give Chelsea a chance in the semi-final. Everyone expected United would deal with them. But Barca showed immense power after all their difficulties in the semi, and they sent United home without the trophy. It was Ronaldo versus Messi—England versus Spain. The match was full of pace and beautiful moves.

United started strongly, with Cristiano having three nice chances in the first ten minutes before Samuel Eto'o scored for Barcelona. From then on, Barca took control, and Messi finished the job with a header in the second half."

David hung his head in his hands.

"A sad game that was," he said. "A sad, sad game."

"So what?" Edo said. "Wasn't that just another *lesson* for Alex Ferguson and Manchester United?"

"Hmm," David mumbled, trying to figure it out. "Not this time."

"What was it then?" Edo asked.

David bounced the ball three times while thinking.

"OK—" he said, finally. "Since time limits us, and Ferguson's United were as close to a perfect system as possible, their losses to Barcelona were *no longer* lessons by that point."

Edo scrunched his face up in curiosity.

"What were they then, David?" he said.

"They were exceptions to the rule!" David said.

"What rule?" said Edo, shaking his head.

David took another one of his long breaths.

"Man United defeats against Barcelona were an *exception*," he said. "They proved the rule that hundreds and hundreds of lessons are *necessary* to create a perfect system. So when something is as close to a perfect system as Ferguson's United were, defeats are no longer lessons but evidence that *hundreds* of defeats are necessary to become a perfect system. Because without the loss—exception—there wouldn't be growth—rule. And therefore, there wouldn't be the perfect system rule."

"A bit stretched, man," said Edo.

David took a big cold sniff.

"But then again, it might all be due to Ronaldo!" he said.

Pessimism—Fear of Living

When Identification Takes Hold of Life

Edo lay on the cold grass. The sun was rapidly descending behind the hill, and he was getting chilly. David was still doing some tricks, although the ball was becoming less visible as the night made its first outlines. He turned to face his friend and squinted.

“Sir Alex Ferguson retired from managing Manchester United almost ten years ago,” David said. “Since then, it has been generally pessimistic for us.” He patted the Manchester United badge on his chest longingly.

“Pessimistic?” said Edo, seeming surprised by David’s choice of the word. “Why so?”

David thought deeply about this.

“It is clear we have been on the rough side of history for a while—the results have been avoiding us,” he said.

Edo nodded.

“So it's been an intense lesson-learning period, right? Where has the wisdom gone?”

“True.”

“Because what is pessimism in its essence?” Edo said, gazing up at the emerging crescent moon. “It is an inability to see the full cycle of the learning process.” He sat up and crossed his legs. “If you think about it, pessimists, deep down, don’t see failure as growth. They don’t recognise the learning process in bad situations. As a result, they avoid any situation that could potentially go wrong. But the so-called bad situations come anyway—always. There is no good without bad, no winning without losing, no euphoria without misery."

"Right," said David.

"And then," Edo continued. "Pessimists always fear new situations. And when those situations come—and they certainly do come—the pessimist experiences real fear. That's why pessimists will rarely have the courage to take a big life adventure."

"You *can* see those treated pessimists on adventures, though," said David, laughing. "But you can always recognise them because they are over-hyped about *everything*."

Edo laughed gently.

"Optimists, on the other hand, are generally more adventurous," he said. "They are the opposite of pessimists, so they understand that inevitable falls are necessary for further growth and learning. And when people are unafraid of new situations, they learn from them."

"Optimists do bicycle kicks, don't they?" said David, teasing his friend.

"Yes, I fell and learnt a lesson," said Edo, massaging his hip. "Optimists skydive. They surf and go rafting. Optimists look forward to the challenge. Pessimists don't because they are afraid something bad might happen."

David nodded.

"The ultimate fear is a fear of death," Edo said solemnly. "And those who are afraid of death, do you know what else they are afraid of?"

"What?"

"They are afraid of life, David—of challenging situations—of losing—of growing—of life itself!"

"Wow, so true," said David, impressed by his friend's words. He sat beside Edo and joined him in admiring the beautiful moon.

"But since, David, in football, it is not life that we are scared of, the question that we need to ask is—why are we so afraid of losing? Why can't we recognise the learning process?"

David threw his fists into the air suddenly.

"Because we are Man United, the greatest club of all!" he shouted at the moon.

"Exactly!" said Edo. "The answer comes down to *identification*. We are afraid of losing because defeats compromise that grand image that we have created—*I am Man United*, or even more so, *I am CR7*. We can only nourish those images through victory. We are afraid of losing because, from a very superficial point of view, losing makes these identifications less valuable. That is why a heavily identified person lacks a deep understanding of the process of growth, and why as soon as you, David, start explaining the Man United situation from recent years as *your* situation, you lose awareness of the process. The same goes for Cristiano, who can't allow himself to lose because losing goes completely against the picture he created about himself. In Cristiano's endless chase for glory, he can't recognise the lesson in defeat. That wisdom doesn't have a place in his ego-created reality where only *victory* proves his life worthy of living."

"Maybe he didn't need the lessons after all. He was born to conquer," said David stubbornly.

"Oh, he needed his defeats, David," said Edo. "The fact that he couldn't deal with them is another story."

"Maybe."

"I will quote Jürgen Klopp now," said Edo. "Klopp said that ninety-eight per cent of football is about dealing with losses but still finding joy in the game the next day. Jürgen said, *I've been learning from my mistakes since the beginning. Many, many times, I stepped into the shit as a manager. What can you do? You grab a tissue, clean it off and try to learn from it. Even my greatest triumph as a manager was born from a disaster.*"[6]

"Oh, again with that Liverpool bastard," said David screwing up his runny nose.

Edo got a little irritated.

"Can you try to see him without Man United glasses for once," he said. "Try and appreciate what he has done for football, the league and the club, could you, man?"

David screwed up his whole face now.

"If I d*on't* see him as a Liverpool bastard," he said. "Then I can only see him as a shyster who uses deceptive methods to convince people to follow his ideas. There's something quite tyrannical about him—something very structured and suffocating. He has put himself in the position of a *moral judge* and believes he has the right to judge journalists, pundits, referees, managers or, perhaps, players who chose not to get vaccinated."

"Oh, *now* I see where you are going with this," Edo said. "But ironically enough, that very dictatorial edge you speak of might be crucial in understanding the real depth of his nature and even his winning mentality."

David scratched his head.

"*I am the normal one.* That's what Klopp said to describe himself when he first came to England and signed with Liverpool," David said.[7] "*Too* normal it seems, from the perspective of an overly oppressive society that is often overly structured and suffocating."

"True," said Edo. "Klopp is under the strong influence of society—audience."

"Yeah, and he draws moral values from that society," said David.

"Just as *you* do, really," Edo said calmly. "Klopp *identifies* with people who have been vaccinated and shames those who haven't, while you identify with the Man United badge and shame those who support Liverpool. You both live in your illusions."

David didn't have a counterargument.

"But when you put those moral judgments and ideas of who is better aside," Edo continued. "When you *detach* from social pressures, what remains are two people aware of the process of growth, who learn from their mistakes and who clean off the shit when they step in it. That's all it is."

David looked a little uncertain.

"Seeing life from the optimistic perspective is a personal decision," he said. "It's entirely up to you, isn't it, Edo? It's about whether you choose to be an optimist or a pessimist, right?"

"I guess so," said Edo. "But I believe that decision comes naturally with the occasional detachment from our identifications. In those moments, we see the world clearly and understand the learning process better. We understand the *process of life* more clearly, David. I think that Klopp, beneath all those suffocating concepts, cherishes the beauty of life, and now he is enjoying the fruit of his losses like an absolute winner. The day Klopp's Liverpool won the Champions League in 2019 was pure joy. When they beat Spurs in the final in Madrid, that victory looked *so simple*. Mohamed Salah gave them the lead in the first minutes with a penalty. After that, it was all one-way traffic. In the end, club legend Divock Origi added a second goal to claim the greatest trophy. That was the one night from which Klopp's path to glory was unstoppable. It was unbelievable because two years before that, nobody had even heard of all those players who were suddenly the champions of Europe."

"As with every dictator, he will eventually fall," David said, screwing up his face again as he struggled to listen to the story. "The same things that make a dictator great eventually lead to his downfall."

Edo smiled softly.

"*Whatever* you may think about his methods," he said. "You can't deny that team was something else. It was a pure Klopp masterclass. *He* made all those players what they are today. *He* planted that superhuman chip in their heads. Andrew Robertson, Alexander-Arnold and even the likes of Van Dijk, Henderson, Roberto Firmino, Sadio Mané and Mo Salah all suddenly became the best players in the world. I *never* thought Salah could become what he became under Klopp. I remember him from Roma and Fiorentina as that annoying winger who would *always* miss a clear chance, one versus one, with a keeper. I saw that as a lack of *mental* strength. But Klopp put that cutting-edge mindset in them, turning them into winners. With absolute mental strength, Salah became a goal machine—clear chances, goals outside the box, you name it."

David nodded in reluctant agreement.

"Those were great years for them, there's no doubt about that," he mumbled.

"The semi-finals against Barcelona were on a different level," Edo continued. "Without Salah and Firmino, Liverpool managed to recover from 3-0 down in the first leg to win the second game 4-0."

"Yeah," mumbled David.

Edo pulled himself up into a crouching position.

"Klopp made a proper team with a proper *mentality*," Edo said. "In an interview on one occasion, he said that his team were a bunch of mentality monsters who didn't wait but worked for *the moment.*[8] That Champions League semi against Barcelona was the proof of that."

"Oh, yes," said David. "With a dose of cheekiness as well—to put it politely. Let's not forget the winning goal came after Alexander-Arnold's corner when he tricked the Barcelona defence and crossed for Origi while nobody was watching."

"It was Barcelona's fault!" said Edo. "They should have been *awake*. He caught them asleep. Legends like Origi don't miss that. The goal was simply a result of incredible determination to win the game."

"I suppose," said David, shuffling to his feet.

Edo put his hand on his friend's back.

"They saw the game from a very optimistic perspective that night," he said. "It was nothing like a normal person would see it."

"I'll tell you something very optimistic now," said David, dropping the ball at his feet on the now frosty grass. "Ronaldo will *win* the Premier League this season, with or without lessons learnt. If not in the name of Man United, then in the name of *CR7*. Mark my words!"

PERSPECTIVE

Old Trafford, Manchester
April 2022

◇

It All Starts With the Audience

Bread and Circuses

The season was coming to an end, and Manchester United were hosting Chelsea at their historic ground, Old Trafford. Only ten days before, Manchester United had lost 4-0 to Liverpool at Anfield, with Cristiano Ronaldo missing from the United team following the death of his son during childbirth and the birth of his daughter, who joined the Ronaldo family as the fifth child.

United were sixth in the table, having won only two of their last ten games. Now, against Chelsea, typical Northern clouds somehow symbolically blocked the flow of the sunlight to the pitch at Old Trafford. The atmosphere in the stadium was silent and dumbfounded. Fans were, once again, exhausted by their team's performance.

David and Edo sat behind the goal, somewhere in the middle of the upper deck of the *East Stand*, with a reasonable view of the pitch. It was Edo's first visit to Old Trafford, and he was enjoying himself. The referee blew his half-time whistle with the teams level at 0-0.

"Now I understand why they call this *The Theatre of Dreams*," Edo said to his friend.

"This is so sad," David replied, unable to enjoy the experience. "We could have been down three goals if not for De Gea. We are just rubbish. I don't remember Man United *ever* being so desperate. It's like the players aren't even trying."

"I'm afraid I can't console you, my dear friend," Edo said, trying to hide his joy at simply being present at the great stadium.

"This should have been our season!" said David. "Things were finally coming together last summer. With Ronaldo joining, we were going to be the main title contenders. I wouldn't have dreamt of this in my worst nightmares." He crossed his muscular arms to isolate himself from the rest of the crowd.

"It's alright, man," Edo said as he observed people silently getting up from their seats. "It's 0-0, David. A draw is an okay result against Chelsea."

"A draw is okay for who?" barked David, his eyes widening. "Certainly not for *Manchester United!* Didn't we already establish that, Edo? I mean, look around you. Don't you see it?"

"See what?"

"Audience!" David said, spreading his right arm across toward the *Sir Alex Ferguson Stand* and then pointing to the crowd at the *Sir Bobby Charlton Stand*. "An audience is *never* satisfied with balance, my friend. They are *never* satisfied with sharing points."

Edo's eyes scanned the stadium. The crowd felt destitute and silent.

"Remember my bakery!" David said. "Imagine there is a universe where Arafat and I *share* the customers, and people get good quality sourdough bread whether they enter my place or Arafat's, so it doesn't make a difference to them. Everyone is at peace."

"Go on," said Edo.

"But let's examine another option as well," said David. "Say, I have built my business to the point where I have enough money to buy an oven to make the Shepherd's loaf. Now, instead of sourdough bread, I bake the magnificent Shepherd's loaf. The customers are delighted, and they no longer go to Arafat's bakery but only to mine because they want *better* bread."

"Yeah, that's the thing," Edo said. "People are greedy. Why couldn't they just be satisfied with decent sourdough?"

"Because they are what they are," said David. "And they are greedy for a good reason, my friend!"

"What's the good reason?" said Edo, his eyes still taking in the vastness of the ground.

"You don't *remember*, Edo?" David said, irritation growing in his voice. "*Evolution*, mate. *Progress*, Edo. Since I have all the customers, I earn enough money for a new, amazing electric *dome* oven. So now I'm selling the Shepherd's loaf *all day*, growing my business extensively. But being as intelligent as I am, I realise my ovens are not only capable of baking bread—they are also capable of melting titanium."

"Okay," Edo said, crumpling his eyebrows. "Is that even a real thing, man?"

"Yes, my friend Edo," David said abruptly. "One thing leads to another, and suddenly I start producing titanium spindles, the only part Elon Musk requires for his rocket to fly safely. As a result of my ingenuity, he launches his rocket to Mars and discovers sustainable life for humans to live there."

"Right."

"You see, Edo. *Evolution!*"

Edo was shaking his head subtly.

"But if the world was in balance in the first place, David," he said. "There wouldn't be a need for finding life on Mars. We could live here on Earth in harmony with each other and the planet, too."

"That's true," said David. "But what about football—laws of the game—ego—surviving—audience? Peace might be nice while it lasts, but *no* peace lasts forever. Sooner or later, we face situations that *require* winning and losing—situations that *force* us to grow. And besides, *they* watch you the whole time."

"Who watches you, man?" said Edo, taking out a flask of hot tea and unscrewing the lid.

"Audience, man," David said, shaking his head again. "You're not following me, mate. The audience observe you for ninety minutes—for the whole season—for your whole *career*."

"They *do* watch you, don't they?" Edo said, observing the far side of the ground—the infamous *Stretford End*, where the most fanatic United fans stood.

"Yes," said David, gently. "They follow every step you take. You are on the stage of life, baking bread in front of seventy thousand raucous, bloodthirsty people, and you have to deliver a goddamn Shepherd's loaf and a load of fucking titanium spindles. They don't want sourdough bread. They don't want *one point each*, for god's sake."

Edo poured two plastic cups of tea while nodding wide-eyed. He put away his flask, passed a cup to David and picked up his own, sipping the hot liquid.

David looked down at his tea for a moment without taking a sip.

"It's not only in this country," he said. "Barcelona fans were so demanding. They booed their best players after a few bad games. Xavi Hernández, the absolute legend of the club, a man who lives and breathes Barca philosophy, said that despite being a homegrown player, he had suffered things that crossed the line. In 2003, they called him the *cancer of Barca.* In 2014, after everything he had done for them, they called him *old and good for nothing*. Xavi said *Barca fans are the most difficult in the world.*"[9]

"That's harsh!" said Edo, sipping on his tea.

"You see, Edo. They *don't want* balance. They *don't want* peace. They *don't want* to share the points. They want you to fucking *strike*."

Some Chelsea players returned to the pitch to warm up and David hit his chest aggressively with his fist which caused tea to spill down his front.

Edo laughed at David. He reached into his bag, pulled out a tissue and handed it to David, who wiped the tea from his jacket while still talking.

"And just as Barca fans want you to strike," he said. "I want United to strike Chelsea, just as I want them to destroy Liverpool or Manchester City. I don't want a draw. I'm not happy with 0-0."

Edo held out a small plastic bag, and David dropped the now tea-soaked tissue into it.

"Thanks," said David.

"No problem, man," said Edo, smiling. "And I agree that everything starts with the audience and their perspective of the game. I believe the audience holds the *key to change* and that if we want to start living peacefully, their relationship with the game needs to start reshaping slowly. Their perspective shall shift."

David took a deep swig of tea.

"Hell no!" he yelled, almost spilling his drink again. "Drawing with Liverpool? No thanks. I want United players to *smash* Liverpool players. The more goals, the better. The further away we are from a draw, the better. I don't want to see high-fives. I want to see Klopp enter the dressing room *ashamed* before the final whistle. I don't even want to see a handshake. I want to see Liverpool players going down the tunnel with their heads down, contemplating their lives. I want to see our players walking around the pitch, hugging each other, and singing with fans. I want *five* goals in the back of the Liverpool net. I want to see Scousers going home *depressed.* Do you know what I mean?"

Edo was giving David his full attention.

"Don't you think it is quite bold saying this after Liverpool smacked United 4-0 a few days ago?" he said.

David just sat there with his mouth open for a moment.

"Especially after Liverpool fans made such an extraordinary gesture," Edo continued. "See how they stood up in the seventh minute of the game, giving the absent Cristiano a standing ovation to support him in his days of grief? The *whole* of Anfield stood up and sang *You'll Never Walk Alone* to their biggest rival. It was an act of deep compassion that they could only express when they replaced their identification with the badge with something more profound. For a moment, the perspective of those fans and their opinion of what is important changed—if not permanently, then only for that minute. A significant minute!"

David grimaced in shame and took a mouthful of tea.

"Compassion," Edo repeated, holding up a finger.

With the teams back on the pitch, the stands became full again.

"I still want to *destroy* them," said David as he saw the players.

"Course you do," said Edo, looking around him and lowering his voice. "You want them to feel how you felt last autumn when Liverpool destroyed United right here at Old Trafford 5-0?"

"*Don't* mention that game!" David shouted. "You can mention all the recent blows against Liverpool, but don't mention *that* one. That one hurt like no other."

"Mo Salah scored a hat-trick," Edo said, ignoring David's request. "It was like Liverpool players were playing on the playground against United's under-seventeen squad."

"You better be careful, mate," said David, clapping with the crowd as the players took up their positions again. "That one hurt. You know that, right? Those were tough days for us. And they are still tough."

"It must have hurt Cristiano as well," Edo said, sensing his friend's impatience. "He came back to United to help them win the league, and in the first derby against the biggest rival, his team got embarrassed like never before."

"Yeah."

"Strangely, it wasn't the first time it happened to Cristiano," said Edo. "He experienced something similar when Barcelona beat

Real Madrid 5-0. The Madrid players were so frustrated. Ronaldo pushed Guardiola away, and Carvalho elbowed Messi in his face before Ramos finally knocked out Messi and Puyol. That's how far 5-0 is from peace—from *balance*.

"I bet Barcelona fans weren't booing their players *that* time," said David, calming down. "5-0—humiliating Madrid, whose players didn't even shake hands after the match. It's all you ever wish for."

"Madness," said Edo.

"You see, my friend, the *audience* wanted them to strike. And strike, they *did*!" David said. "They want the Shepherd's loaf, and I'm here to deliver the bread!"

"They want bread and circuses," said Edo, finishing the last of his tea.

"They want," David continued before breaking into laughter. "*Ha*, nice one, Edo. Bread and circuses! *Literally*!"

Romance or Technology

It Was Different Back in the 1930s

"Come here, you big angry geezer," said Edo, slinging his right arm around David's neck. "Let's take a selfie for my first time at this great stadium."

Edo took a few and continued to shift the angle of his phone.

"Okay, how many selfies do you need?" David said in frustration. "I'm not in the mood, my friend."

"Come on, man," said Edo, making funny faces for the camera. "Let's try it from a different perspective."

"Let me watch the game now," David said, forced a smile and escaping Edo's grip. "Whose shot on goal was that? You see, now I missed the action!"

"No idea," Edo muttered.

"You don't even care," David said, glancing at Edo, who was occupied with his phone.

"Mason Mount left footed shot from outside the box is close but misses to the right. Assisted by Kai Havertz," Edo said, reading the action from his phone and grinning proudly.

"Oh, right. Thanks!" said David.

Edo held up his phone, showing David a picture of them.

"Man, let me publish this photo of the two of us on Instagram," he said.

"Oh, freaking Instagram! We were wiser before Instagram and Facebook and all the rest of those," said David before yelling obscenities at the referee.

"Probably, yeah," said Edo. "But on the other hand, there's so much *information* available these days. We are learning *a lot*."

"Yeah, there's information," David agreed without taking his eye off the game. "But what kind of information?"

"All kinds of information."

"Most of it is fake!" David insisted. "Just like that photo you just published on Instagram. My smile was fake in that photo. You know that, right?"

Edo thought about it for a moment.

"You're right," he said. "Technology is a bit out of control at this point, David. "More precisely, people are not *in* control of technology, but rather *it* controls *them*."

"No control whatsoever," David said before standing suddenly as United almost scored, then sitting immediately. "Technology kills romance, the most important ideal we seek in football. Think of the first World Cup in 1930."

"That was a long time ago, man," said Edo. "But what about it?"

"Just the sheer romance of it, my friend—the national team of Yugoslavia, for instance. Imagine a group of semi-professionals who earned money at mills, bakeries, that kind of thing—a bunch of tough guys with bruised hands travelling to the end of the world, to Uruguay." David finally put a genuine smile on his face. "They departed from Belgrade, where a train took them to Marseille. Then, they boarded a steamboat in Marseille to travel to Montevideo."

"Sounds entertaining," said Edo.

"Indeed," said David. "The team spent a couple of weeks on the boat, training on the deck. With limited space to train, there was unlimited time for something to go wrong—alcohol, ladies, fights, showing off. Their star player, Blagoje Moša Marjanović, almost died due to food poisoning."

"Oh yeah?" said Edo. "It *is* an interesting story, but why are you telling me it, David?"

"It was romantic, that's why," said David, finishing the last of his tea and throwing the cup into Edo's plastic bag. "It was way before technology. When they arrived in Uruguay after weeks on the sea, they didn't have phones to snap selfies all day. They put on their best attire with good hats on their heads and cigarettes in their mouths and they went to party hard instead. They knew what to do and where to go instinctively without the help of Google."

"Good story, David," said Edo, smiling, and David continued.

"When the team had screwed up everything they possibly could," he said. "Their coach, Boško Simonović, made his legendary statement: *Unlike life, in football, there is always a second half*—to fix what can be fixed, right?[10] And fix it, they did! In the opening match, they beat mighty Brazil—the most powerful team in the world at that point."

"Bless them," Edo said with a laugh.

"Bless them, indeed," said David. "Aleksandar Tirnanić, called Tirke, scored the first goal in the game. The referee blew the whistle to signify the goal, and Tirke looked confused as if he was thinking, *Did I score against Brazil?*"

"How can you possibly know all that?" said Edo.

"Oh, I watched the movie about it," said David, crouching and clenching his fists as United ran at the Chelsea goal again.

"Oh, you watched the movie, huh? Technology?" said Edo.

"Yeah," said David, scratching his bald scalp and sighing as the ball ended up in the arms of the Chelsea goalkeeper. "However, the next morning, people in Yugoslavia were waiting nervously for a postman to deliver the news. People didn't have phones, TV or radio. The barber, baker, and policeman were *all* waiting for the news. Everyone stopped momentarily when the newspaper finally arrived with a big headline: *Yugoslavia 2-1 Brazil*. Their Tirke had smashed Brazil. The party had begun. So romantic!"

"Times have changed," said Edo solemnly.

"Yeah, today, technology kills romance," said David. "Just look at that bloody VAR system that takes the piss for two-millimetre offsides. It was much more convenient when a ref would allow a goal because *the striker always had an advantage*. A two-millimetre offside used to be onside. They were romantic times, Edo!"

Edo nodded his semi-agreement.

"I see benefits of technology," he said. "But until we learn to control technology, it will play with our minds—and players' minds and coaches' minds too, for that matter. Three years ago, in April 2019, Manchester City played the quarter-final of the Champions League against Spurs. In stoppage time, Sergio Agüero passed the ball from the right side to Raheem Sterling, who received it in the box. Sterling faked the shot to shake off Alderweireld and Davies before firing the ball next to Sánchez and placing it behind the heartbroken Spurs keeper, Hugo Lloris. The Spurs manager, Mauricio Pochettino, was cursing, and Guardiola's City were finally into the semi-finals of the Champions League! Following three years of dedication, a mighty approach and brilliant football, Pep Guardiola finally achieved what he was brought into City for. The Spaniard was delirious—certain that he was *the chosen one* and could go all the way to lift the trophy. Sterling's teammates chased him towards the stands, where fans received them with open arms, letting go of painful previous seasons' debacles and experiencing a collective metamorphosis from the wounded caterpillar into the stunning European butterfly. Afterwards, Sterling walked back across the pitch, raising his hands to the sky as if to say, *Take me, I'm Yours!'*

"City don't deserve it!" said David suddenly, his frustration growing from United's lack of opportunities on the field before him.

"But! Wait a moment," said Edo. "It's not over yet. There's *more* drama. The referee, Cüneyt Çakır, receives a message from somebody in the VAR room. Agüero was *offside* before he passed the ball to Sterling. *No goal, offside,* shows on a big screen.

"You see—damn technology," said David, looking at his friend briefly.

"Pep was kneeling on the pitch with tragedy in his eyes," said Edo. "The man was in heaven for a whole minute, and then this. He was broken. Such a rollercoaster of extreme emotions *must* leave some mark on you, right? Technology can create mental cases if it's not under control."

"And yet, it has taken the romance away," David said, squinting into the grey rainy sky above Manchester.

Edo looked at the sky as well. The roof of the old stadium was leaking, so they were getting wet despite being undercover.

"In the end, the Yugoslavian players reached the semi-final of the World Cup against the home team Uruguay," David said.

"Right," said Edo, remembering David's previous story.

"In that game, the referee made several mistakes that tore Yugoslavia apart, including a disallowed goal for no reason," David recalled. "*We didn't play against eleven players—not even against twelve. We played against thirteen, fourteen or maybe even fifteen players.* That's what the Yugoslavian Blagoje Marjanović said after the match."

Edo lost himself in thoughts for a moment.

"If VAR was operating back then," he said. "Maybe Marjanović wouldn't have needed to say something like that."

"Maybe," said David. "One incident, however, has remained in the history books more than the others. In the thirty-first minute of the match, the ball went out of play and was hoofed straight back on by a policeman. Peregrino Anselmo of Uruguay received it and scored a goal. A Yugoslavian player grabbed the policeman by his neck, and guards surrounded the player, wanting to take him off the pitch."[11]

"And you still think it was better without technology?" said Edo.

"Well, my friend," said David, looking Edo in the eyes. "Maybe I'm crazy, but it sounds romantic to me."

"Romance!" David yelled. "*That's* what it's about."

"Chelsea are in trouble!" Edo said as United began to pressure the Chelsea defence.

"Are you serious?" David said in confusion. "We can't do *anything* to them. We are blunt."

"I'm not talking about this match," said Edo, glancing over at the lower deck where some three thousand Chelsea supporters were squeezing into the South-East corner. "Chelsea are about to undergo massive change as Roman Abramovich is forced to sell the club due to his ties with Vladimir Putin.

"Oh yeah," said David.

"But hey! Challenging times often turn out to be the most romantic times," Edo said.

"Oh yeah?" repeated David.

"Yeah, man. Take, for example, the Chelsea squad from the pandemic 2019/20 season—Lampard's *inaugural* season. Just before Frank Lampard was appointed manager, Chelsea were hit with a transfer ban, meaning they could not buy new players for two transfer windows—something unheard of at that point."

"I remember," David said, cheering up and finding a sudden interest in the conversation. "And we are talking about *Chelsea* here—the club known for big, juicy transfers—a club that had been making nasty transfers summer after summer for almost two decades since Abramovich took over the club. Didier Drogba joined the club for thirty-five million pounds during the first

Mourinho spell back when thirty-five million *meant* thirty-five million. Andriy Shevchenko came in 2006 for forty million pounds. At that point, they bought Fernando Torres for fifty-three million pounds in the most expensive transfer in Premier League history. Then Álvaro Morata came in for sixty million pounds in 2017 and so on. Kepa Arrizabalaga cost seventy-one million pounds in 2018 to become the most expensive goalkeeper ever. That one proved to be very bizarre."

"All very true," said Edo. "Chelsea later appealed, getting the ban reduced to a single transfer window. But at the beginning of that season, it seemed like game over—like an *unsolvable* situation. The situation left Chelsea out in the cold without their most powerful tool. It was a *tragedy*!"

"Exactly. A tragedy!" said David, leaning forward to get closer to the action.

"Do you remember what position Chelsea finished that season, though?" Edo asked.

David scratched his head and thought.

"I believe they finished fourth, just behind us."

"That's correct!" said Edo. "On the same points as Man United as well. And allow me to say this—Manchester United were pretty solid that season, whereas Liverpool and City were on a different level."

"Yeah, it was a decent season," said David. "That was Ole Gunnar Solskjær's first full season in charge. Ole, come back! We didn't appreciate you enough! This guy is just clueless," David pointed towards the bench where the United manager Ralf Rangnick was sitting. "He can't coach Ronaldo!"

"I am trying to say that Chelsea played wonderfully that season."

"I see Chelsea left a mark on you that year," said David sarcastically. "Maybe you should be sitting over there?" He pointed over at the Chelsea fans.

"Yup," said Edo, laughing. "That season, Chelsea proved that the romance is still alive and that difficult times bring great romances. Even though Chelsea seemed lost and defeated before the season kicked off, once the campaign started, they released the magic."

"Did you like it that much?" David asked, facing his friend briefly. "I was too occupied with United, who did way better than expected. And, of course, with Leicester, who had yet another mad start to the season."

"Okay, Chelsea might not have been *that* miraculous," Edo said, lowering his voice. "But it *was* quite romantic. They took a bunch of Chelsea academy kids and other youngsters back off loan from various clubs, and these kids were suddenly leading the great Chelsea toward the Champions League. Appointing Lampard was a wise move, considering the situation Chelsea were in. They were young players, and he was a young coach. He certainly knew how to manage them."

"It didn't seem so after the first match of the season when we demolished them 4-0. Bam, bam, bam! What a start that was," David said, throwing his fists out.

"True," said Edo. "But Chelsea were quite unlucky then. They hit the woodwork on a couple of occasions. After that match, it started, though. Tammy Abraham and Mason Mount, two players aged twenty-one and twenty at that point, came alive. Chelsea brought these two young players home who would have probably *never* got the opportunity to start if there had not been a transfer ban. They scored sixteen goals between them in the next fourteen Premier League matches after that defeat to United."

"That was some start for them, indeed," said David.

"That was romance if you like! It was just full of youth, energy, positivity," said Edo.

"I suppose," said David with a frown.

"In the meantime, Mason Mount has become one of the world's most valuable players and won the Champions League," Edo continued. "And it all started with that transfer ban. That is proof that good doesn't exist without bad, David. And the opposite, too. Every bad situation creates good situations, and every good situation creates bad situations."

David leapt to his feet as United once more ran toward the Chelsea goal before being dispossessed. He sat down again.

"If that's the case, Edo, then one must refer to the game as *the tragic game of football*!"

"The tragic game of football?" said Edo.

"Yes, mate," said David. "We often say football is the *beautiful* game. But as you say, it's always a *tragic* game for a losing team. It all comes down to perspective—how will you see the situation, negatively or positively? And as a *lesson* or as a *defeat*?"

Edo nodded, impressed at his friend's words.

"Exactly, David. And equally important is to understand other people's perspectives, too. Or at least to not think yours is the only correct one. You remember? Compassion!"

"Compassion—" David muttered.

"Do you remember the epic match between Chelsea and Ajax in the Champions League group stage from the same season?" Edo asked.

"The crazy game at Stamford Bridge that ended 4-4?" said David.

"Yes! Balance! 4-4," said Edo.

David rolled his eyes.

"But that's not the point right now," Edo said. "Do you remember that hilarious Kepa Arrizabalaga own goal when the ball bounced off the post straight into his face before it went in?"

David nodded enthusiastically without taking his eyes off the game.

"You mean that amazing Hakim Ziyech free kick for Ajax when he scored from an impossible angle, and on the way, the ball hit Kepa in the face?" he said.

David and Edo looked at each other briefly.

"You see, there are always two perspectives to every story," David said. "You saw it as a hilarious own goal, and I saw it as a spectacular free kick. There are always positive and negative ways to see things. I saw it as something amazing, and you saw it as something hilarious."

"That's right, there are different perspectives," said Edo. "But can you really claim to know which is positive and which is negative? José Mourinho once said that every goal is someone's mistake and that you can't concede a goal if at least one of your players didn't make a mistake. On the other hand, ask Guardiola about that, and you would probably get the answer that every goal includes unbelievable team effort."

"Mourinho is right in the end," said David. "You know how they say, *The man who does things makes many mistakes*. So it's quite normal that those who play football will make mistakes. The point is to move forward and learn from them!"

"I didn't say he's wrong," said Edo. "But there *is* another perspective. And let's face it, the world would be bleak if there were no perspective opposite to the one Mourinho sees the world through."

"What does that mean?" David looked at Edo uncomfortably.

"Well, let's say Mourinho likes to see the world *negatively*," said Edo.

"Maybe," said David. "But hasn't he done some amazing things with his *negative* perspective?"

"Okay, let's not talk about Mourinho," said Edo. "I wanted to say that sometimes it's worth changing perspective on a particular matter. Even when it comes to your own thoughts, changing perspective and seeing them from another perspective can be useful. If some important people throughout history were ready to change their perspective on certain issues, we could have avoided many devastating wars."

"True," said David.

"And the same thing applies to emotions," Edo said. "We can even change perspective on our emotions."

"Please elaborate, mate," said David, bored by the game.

"Sure," said Edo. "You know how football players get *excited* when playing in the big scene?"

"Yeah."

"And you know how some players get *nervous* instead?"

“I suppose.”

“Physically, it’s the same thing, David. Both emotions make your heart race and your hands sweaty. But you can change perspective—to change the thoughts that colour those emotions—to see your feelings as *excitement* rather than *nervousness*.”

“Yes!” said David, excitedly. “That way, we add a positive mental concept to our physical state and see our sweaty hands as something positive. One sets you for positive performance, and one cuts your wings off negatively. Excitement is something top footballers have ingrained in their winning mentality.”

“You see,” said Edo. “You can even change the perspective of your emotions. *Tragedy* is simply a state of mind.”

José, The Special One, Mourinho

A Relic of the Past

"Roman Abramovich will go down in Chelsea history as the greatest owner the club has had," announced Edo to his big friend, who was now visually irritated by his team's performance.

"Yeah, most of which he owes to Mourinho—he is the one who made Abramovich's era great," said David abruptly.

"I kindly asked you *not* to mention Mourinho," Edo said. "But if you insist, I do believe Mourinho is a good example of a man who *struggles* to change perspective."

"Don't shit on Mourinho!" David shouted. "He was the last manager to bring trophies to Man United as well. Show some respect!"

"I am not shitting on Mourinho, man," said Edo defensively. "I'm just *noticing*."

"You are noticing my *ass*," David said, punching Edo on his shoulder.

"You see," said Edo, rubbing his shoulder. "*This* is what happens when you can't see another perspective. You become aggressive. You become Mourinho-esque."

"Why would Mourinho need to change his perspective?" said David. "He is missing *nothing* in his life."

"Well, he might be missing understanding for other people," said Edo. "Just as you do. If you don't try to understand other people's perspectives, then those people become your enemies. If you identify with your perspective so much, you lose compassion for others and can't make strong relationships. You remember, strong *identification* means strong *ego*. A strong ego equals a lack of compassion. And *that's* why Mourinho has had so many difficult relationships with players. In other words, he doesn't relate to players."

David shook his head.

"If Mourinho doesn't relate to players, who does?" he said.

Edo thought for a moment before speaking.

"Ander Herrera said, *Mourinho is the best manager in the world—when things go well.*[12] I believe the problem is he can't spot when things go bad with players—when the players go bad."

"Wrong," said David, suddenly. "Mourinho has made some world-class players out of decent players. Diego Milito, Didier Drogba, Mesut Özil, Nemanja Matić, John Terry, Javier Zanetti, and Frank Lampard, to name a few. If Mourinho didn't exist, Lampard wouldn't have ended his career as one of the greatest, and he certainly wouldn't have got to manage Chelsea at the age of forty-one."

"Look," said Edo. "José *has* made world great players out of *brilliant* players, *not* out of decent players. There's a big difference. How many brilliant players has he *ruined*, like Paul Pogba, Iker Casillas, Bastian Schweinsteiger, and Juan Mata? And why? Because José has a big *ego* problem. He couldn't stand that there was a bigger superstar than himself in the dressing room. I mean, what are we talking about? At his first press conference ever in England, he said, *I think I am The Special One*."[13]

"That's because he *is* The Special One," David barked. "There have been *so many* games throughout his career that proved that.

Remember when he managed Inter Milan in the first leg of the Champions League semi-finals against Barcelona in 2010 at San Siro? Sneijder, Maicon and Milito all got on the scoresheet. The final score was 3-1. Inter destroyed Barcelona, the mightiest of them all at that point."

"Still," mumbled Edo. "An ego problem."

David scowled and turned to face his friend.

"Tell me Edo," David said. "How many world-class players have followed him to different countries just to be coached by him—by that ego? Ricardo Carvalho, Michael Essien, Samuel Eto'o, Zlatan Ibrahimović, for God's sake! They were ready to *die* for him."

"Okay, well, I agree with that, David, but how many absolute talents has he *not* recognised and let them go? Mohamed Salah, Kevin De Bruyne, Romelu Lukaku all got missed. José doesn't have a good record of developing young players."

"He has a good trophy record, though," said David. "Two Champions League titles for starters. Also, a UEFA Cup, the Europa League, three Premier League titles, two Serie A titles, one La Liga title, two Portuguese Premier Liga trophies, cups, cups, and more cups. The man won *three* trophies for Man United, but sadly, we didn't appreciate that enough!"

"Maybe so," said Edo. "But he refused to shake hands with Pep Guardiola after Barcelona humiliated him 5-0 in his first season as a manager of Real Madrid." Edo was also uncharacteristically raising his voice now. "Mourinho did his best to stop Messi from scoring, but then Xavi, Pedro, Villa twice and Jeffrén sunk his Real."

“Mourinho won the Champions League with Porto!” David yelled back. “Mourinho—and let this sink in—holds the record of a hundred and fifty home matches *undefeated* across nine years with four different clubs. In his *first* year at Chelsea, he won the Premier League while conceding fifteen goals! *Fifteen*! His Chelsea were bulletproof.”

Edo paused for a moment.

“That’s remarkable, I must admit,” he said.

“If he had a bakery,” said David. “He would have some *special* bread there. It would be a special bakery!”

Edo nodded, acknowledging again the excellent record before continuing.

“They sacked José from Chelsea twice,” he said. “They sacked him from Real Madrid, Man United, and Spurs. He did not leave on good terms from Madrid, Chelsea, United or Tottenham.”

“He did leave in a good spirit from Inter and Porto, though,” said David. “Players were crying for him *not* to leave.”

“The likes of *Materazzi* cried, you mean,” Edo said. “The two bonded well, attracting each other’s misery and pain.”

David shook his head both at the statement and the game.

“Mourinho believes his way is the only right way,” said Edo. “He gave Pogba a pretty hard time at United.”

“Yeah,” said David. “Because he had a problem with Pogba's attitude.”

“More than anything,” said Edo. “He was annoyed by Pogba's funny haircuts, which is further proof that Mourinho is living in the past. It’s the twenty first century—a time of diversity! We should celebrate differences and learn to deal with them, rather than judge them. José is simply unable to manage a person or situation which is just a bit out of the box—out of his field of perception. He is also unable to follow the evolution of football, and the evolution of society, for that matter. But it is the same thing, isn't it? And that's why he was *The Special One* for almost twenty years. Not anymore, though."

"Football is life, indeed," said David, defiantly. "And it would be nothing without Mourinho."

"Exactly, football *is* life," said Edo. "If you can't follow the societal trends, you can't follow football trends either. If you can't accept different hairstyles in 2018—the year that José had the spat with Pogba—you can't accept the changes in strategic approach to the game either. Mourinho is stuck in the past. This is a time of big changes, and if we can't appreciate differences, then we can't move forward. Not only does José fail to understand different perspectives, but he despises them, he hates differences and authenticity."

"He is the boss!" said David, holding an authoritative finger in the air.

"He might have built a special bakery with special bread, but there is no diversity among his breads," said Edo.

"He strives for *order*, and players who also strive for order do well under José," said David. "Mourinho quoted Kobe Bryant on one occasion, saying, *People say I'm difficult, but I'm only difficult for the ones that don't share my principles*."[14]

"Well, exactly!" said Edo. "I mean, he fought with the likes of Casillas, Pogba and Schweinsteiger. Do you think they didn't have their principles? I can assure you they did. They probably just had a different perspective on some things, and Mourinho couldn't handle that."

"Yeah, I don't know about that, my friend." said David. "Mourinho is the best!"

Edo leaned in closer to David.

"*I am José Mourinho, and I don't change. I arrive with all my qualities and my defects*. That's what José said when he joined Real Madrid," said Edo.[15] "How arrogant! I'm sorry to say it, but do you know who doesn't change, David? Unwise people, that's who. Unwise people do not change!"

David shook his head and held up his finger again.

"José was right to say that since he joined Real after his major treble success with Inter," David said. "You need to give him credit, though. He's changed a lot since then. When he joined Spurs, he said he would not make the same mistakes from the past but would rather be making new ones."

"Ok," said Edo, tilting his head in acknowledgement. "That *is* a big step for him, indeed!"

"One thing is clear. There is *no* middle ground with Mourinho," said David. "You either love him or hate him."

"Well," said Edo. "It's just a matter from whose perspective you look at him—Pogba's or Zlatan's perhaps. Pogba couldn't stand being in the same room as him, while Zlatan said he was ready to die for him at Inter."[16]

David nodded.

"Mourinho is now in Roma!" he said, excitedly. "It's amazing that he brought Abraham from Chelsea. The one who was discovered by Lampard will get Mourinho back to winning ways. Mou loves his strikers! They are going to win a trophy together. Mark my words!"

"Mourinho won the Premier League title in both spells at Chelsea!" David continued.

"Yes, alright!" Edo conceded. "Mou has been *alright.*"

"And Chelsea fans were *happy with him* during both of his spells at the club," David said. "And that's all you really need."

"Interestingly, fans were also happy with Lampard's first season in charge," said Edo. "Although it was a *very* different atmosphere in the club compared to Mou's era. Lampard's Chelsea were not title contenders, which tells us that fans can be happy even when their prime motivation for happiness is not victories but peace, togetherness, and romance—when the prime motivation is not making the Shepherd's loaf, but making nice, soft bagels with your pals."

David rolled his eyes and laughed.

"They were doing well under Lampard," Edo continued. "But it wasn't just Abraham and Mount who were doing well. Others were also taking part—Reece James, Fikayo Tomori and Callum Hudson-Odoi, who was only eighteen when the campaign launched. They were *all* doing well."

"That was a young squad!" said David.

"I remember the League Cup game against Grimsby Town," said Edo. "It was the beginning of the season when Lampard gave Reece James and Callum Hudson-Odoi an opportunity, considering they were up against a League Two side. That was both of their debuts that season, and they both scored in a big 7-1 victory."

"It was just a League Two side, though," said David. "So the match was insignificant."

"Insignificant?" Edo said, raising his voice. "It might have been insignificant for you and me. But for those two lads, it was the World Cup final. Those youngsters had *everything* to fight for. And other youngsters started, such as Marc Guéhi and Billy Gilmour, who also played well."

David nodded.

"You see," said Edo. "Even though sometimes a certain match seems insignificant, try to change the perspective, and suddenly you have a World Cup final to watch. Try to put yourself in those guys' shoes—that's the *true* meaning of empathy."

"Interesting!" muttered David.

"Because, *yes*, football is life, football is the universe," Edo continued. "But just as football is the universe, every match is a universe unto itself."

David thought about it for a second.

"True," he said. "With winners and losers—with happiness and sadness—with *lessons* to learn."

Edo turned and smiled at David, who refused to take his eyes off the game.

"And every single player is a universe unto himself," Edo said. "And on that day, those youngsters got to add something big into their universes. And trust me, although the match seemed irrelevant, and they were only playing Grimsby Town, all those kids there on the pitch were universes unto themselves, trying to *make* it important."

"True as well," said David. "And the best part is that they *made* it important. Because they were doing well, and they were scoring goals."

"Yeah," said Edo. "Imagine what it meant for Hudson-Odoi to score the first goal that season after all the hype and expectation he had to live with during the summer. *Imagine* what it meant for James to score on his debut for Chelsea while playing as a right-back. Every single goal is a universe unto itself as well."

"Right, and look at him now," David said, pointing at Reece James as he ran from the full-back position to receive the ball at the edge of the box. "He's a proper monster—probably the best Chelsea player at the minute."

"Indeed," said Edo. "And it meant the world to Gilmour and Guéhi even though they didn't score. It meant a lot to Michy Batshuayi, who scored twice that night, and Kurt Zouma, who scored his first one since returning to Chelsea. Pedro Rodriguez also scored his first of the season. It was meant to take him a step closer to the starting eleven—perhaps, the last real opportunity in his career to prove himself a proper big player. Do you know who scored the first one of the game?" Edo said excitedly.

"My friend," said David, getting irritated by his friend's insistence on speaking through the match. "Do I *look* like I know who scored the first goal for Chelsea in their 7-1 win against Grimsby Town in the League Cup in 2019?"

Edo smiled, unperturbed by his friend's frustration.

"Among all of those players who were desperate to score," he said. "A man scored who needed it more than anybody else—*Ross Barkley*."

"Why do you say that?" said David.

"Ross Barkley came to Chelsea two years earlier, and he'd been *the one* ever since," said Edo.

"*The one?* What do you mean, Edo?"

"The one to lead Chelsea back to glory," said Edo. "The one to embody the spirit of the club—the *new* Frank Lampard. Barkley had not been able to live up to expectations. The pressure was too much."

"And then the *real* Lampard came?" said David.

"Exactly," said Edo. "Then Lampard came as a manager! And the pressure hit its ceiling." Edo gazed at the grey sky, still pouring rain. "Everybody put Barkley in Lampard's shoes, thus *also* putting pressure on the manager by saying that Lampard would know how to manage and mould Barkley in his own image."

David nodded.

"But it didn't happen," Edo continued. "Barkley was not doing well. He couldn't score despite playing most games at the beginning of the season."

"Lampard pushed him, didn't he?" said David.

"Yes, man," said Edo. "And the frustration grew after every match, both for Barkley *and* Lampard. The situation came to a head in the first round of the Champions League during a 1-0 loss to Valencia. In the last few minutes of the game, Chelsea won a penalty, and Barkley stepped up to take it, pushing the regular takers Jorginho and Willian away from the ball with confidence, and who could blame him? It was his moment."

"Right!" said David." Barkley missed, didn't he?"

"He hit the bar!" said Edo. "It took the collective frustration to the next level, and the negativity started to penetrate the fanbase. They didn't want him starting anymore. Then the Grimsby match came, and Barkley had another chance, perhaps his *last* one. And after four minutes, the man scored."

"He must have been relieved."

"Everyone was relieved, I think," said Edo. "Barkley got the ball twenty-five meters from goal, passed a defender and scored in the low left corner. I mean, it was Grimsby—not the strongest defensive line. It's not like he could pass through Virgil van Dijk like that. But the goal counted, and he needed one more than anything."

"From his perspective, it was like a World Cup winner," David said.

"It was, David. For Barkley and other guys, that game *meant* the world, and therefore it *was* the world. Sometimes in life, you might not be willing to do something because it seems irrelevant or insignificant. Change the perspective, and you have a world of opportunity in your palm."

"And there we go," said David as Reece James got the ball in acres of space. "He's got all the time in the world now—"

Kai Havertz flicked James's cross for Marcos Alonso, who slammed the ball past De Gea into the roof of the United net.

"Goal!" said Edo, standing up and instantly sitting down, remembering he was in the United section. "Sorry," he said.

"It was coming," said David, his head in his hands. "We are awful."

"Wow, what a nice volley that was!" Edo said.

"Nice?" David asked and crossed his arms. "I wish I could change perspective and see it as something nice."

You Can't Fake the Touch

Gently, Intimately, Tenderly.

"United can't get hold of the ball," David said as the Chelsea song resounded around Old Trafford. "We are not being *intimate* with the ball!"

"Intimate?" said Edo, surprised by the word.

"I took that one from Miroslav Ćiro Blažević," David said, distracting himself from the situation on the pitch.

"Ćiro—of course!" said Edo. "The coach who led Croatia to the bronze medal in the 1998 World Cup in France."

"Ćiro was obsessed with touch," said David. "He always taught his players to be *intimate* with the ball. *Entirely intimate,* he would say. That was his philosophy."[17]

"I believe, though—" said Edo. "He was the type of coach who cared more about aesthetics and image—about the surface of things—than he cared about the depth of football. In other words—a *charlatan—a faker*. But an absolute icon, nonetheless!"

"I don't think you can fake a touch," said David.

"Well, you got me there," said Edo, smiling.

"Think of the first touch!" said David. "The first touch is the most important thing in football, right? If you have a *gentle* first touch—if you do it right and send the ball to the right place, no defender or goalkeeper can handle it. It tears them apart. It breaks the patterns and rules they have learnt in a football academy. It breaks the *game*. First touch is a game-changer. It's like putting defenders on thin ice. It hurts them! Take, for instance, Zinedine Zidane! I will never forget his first touch.

When he received the ball with that elegance, the man marking him would tremble, and the remaining twenty players would also tremble along with him—right across the pitch."

"Nicely said, David," conceded Edo.

"A lousy first touch is the complete opposite," said David. "Some of the worst injuries come from a lousy first touch—when players want to regain control, and in that attempt, they make doomed and uncontrolled tackles."

The Chelsea fans sang even louder as the game restarted from the centre. David shook his head, turning away from the pitch.

"And you know where the first touch is equally important?" he said.

"Tell me," said Edo.

"In life!" said David. "My mother calls it *the first impression*. She always told me the first impression is the most important. If you do it wrong, you don't get another opportunity. *You only get one chance to leave a first impression, David*, she would tell me. If you do it right, you open every door to yourself and pave your path with gold, whether in a job interview, on a first date, establishing a bakery, writing a book, or—"

"Or in the box in the ninety-fourth minute," Edo interrupted. "When your life depends on how you receive the ball."

"Ninety-fourth minute?" said David. "Who are you talking about? Surely, not—"

"AGÜEROOOO," Edo shouted suddenly, to the disgust of the United fans around them. "Sergio Agüero, my friend," he confirmed.

"Oh, you *bastard*," David said solemnly. "Thanks for bringing that up."

"He needed that first touch to be exquisite," said Edo. "He needed that first touch to *do the job* for him. He just needed the first touch, and everything else would unfold naturally. The year was 2012. Manchester City were playing QPR in the last game of the season."

"I know this, Edo," David said, irritated. "Why are you—"

"The result was 2-2 in stoppage time," Edo interrupted. "City needed a goal to claim their first title after forty-four years of waiting. Balotelli passed the ball into the box, and time stood still for City fans. It was the last chance of the match—their last chance of claiming the title and leaving Manchester United and Alex Ferguson behind. Agüero received the ball in the box. It was an easy pass to receive, but *no* pass is truly easy under those circumstances. Agüero took a good first touch, left the defender on the ground, opened a corridor to goal for himself and smashed the ball as hard as he could."

David said nothing.

"The scenes were out of this world!" Edo said.

"Now that I think about it," said David. "Although I agree with my mother that the first impression is important, I don't agree it is the most *important* thing. Yes, we tried to present our bakery as well as possible when we first opened. But you know what got customers buying bread? It wasn't the first impression. It was the *quality* of the bread."

"Yeah?" said Edo.

"Let's be honest. You don't judge a book by its cover," said David. "You don't judge a bread by its crust, nor a footballer by their first touch." David's eyes widened as Cristiano Ronaldo tried to open up the space for a new counterattack. "First touch *is* important, my friend. But try to think of a few good footballers who had a great first touch—apart from Zidane."

"Okay," said Edo. "Özil, Iniesta, Phil Foden!" he yelled. "Foden is the *new* Zidane!"

"Exactly," said David. "Özil, Iniesta—They've *all* got the first touch, but first touch is not the primary thing you associate with them. They're *complete* players with an immense depth of talent. So *first touch* or *first impression* is just the cherry on top—a final note in the melody. It's the top of an iceberg—the part we see above water. There's so much more underwater, without which the top of the iceberg wouldn't even be there. It's impossible to leave a deep, genuine, authentic first impression anywhere if you are not decent overall."

Edo thought for a moment.

"In my opinion," he said, "*Nobody* is as intimate with the ball as Paul Pogba."

"What?" said David, looking a little shocked. "And where did that come from? He is very overrated!"

"And I'm talking *real* intimate," said Edo, ignoring the question. "As intimate as Ćiro could have only dreamed of. It's just *different* when he touches the ball. It's—it's—" Edo rolled his hands as if searching for the perfect word. "It's *poetry,*" he said.

David shook his head in disbelief.

"Why on earth would you say such a thing?" he said.

"I guess it just reminds me of the perfect harmony," said Edo, tilting his head. "It looks so effortless when Pogba dribbles with his long legs. It's as if he controls more muscles of his legs and feet than anybody else. It's like he's doing it in slow motion but still *so* effectively. There's some serious *composure* in those legs, David."

"Sounds like *someone* has a thing for Pogba!" said David.

"I just love his style of playing," Edo admitted. "And there's his pass, which seems he is using just his foot without the rest of the leg. It's simply *beautiful* to watch. Such a shame he has an injury at the moment."

"He's a talent, I agree," said David. "But not much more than that. Pogba never justified his price tag. He was solid at Juventus but hasn't done much for us."

"I think he's done a lot," Edo argued. "And I also think Mourinho didn't know how to let his talent flourish when coaching him here at Man United."

"I am *not* going *there* again," said David, raising his voice.

"Yep, sorry!" said Edo.

David leaned forward into the game.

"And look, I'm not entirely sure Ćiro would want Pogba in his team," David said. "I can't deny that Ćiro had some very intimate players himself. Robert Prosinečki was intimate as fuck with the ball, not to mention Davor Šuker. His goal against Denmark during Euro 1996 sums up the importance of the first touch. Šuker said in the decades following that legendary goal that the essence of the goal was *not* his chip over the head of Peter Schmeichel, the best goalkeeper in the world. It was Šuker's incredible first touch when he received the long ball, which gave him the time and space to confront Schmeichel one-on-one and deliver that epic chip."[18]

"Ćiro taught him well, I guess," said Edo.

"And he has come to the rescue again," David shouted, suddenly standing up and applauding formally without much intensity as Cristiano Ronaldo scored United's equaliser just two minutes after the Chelsea goal. "He's the *only* player worthy of wearing the United shirt this season," David announced. "At the age of thirty-seven he just keeps banging them in despite the horrendous form of the rest of the team."

"That *was* a quality finish!" Edo admitted, joining in with the applause. "But that first touch made *all* the difference. He received it so well with his right foot before he volleyed it in!"

"Surely, you can't fake that, my friend!" David said, wide-eyed at his team getting back into the game.

"Absolutely," said Edo.

"Well done, Ronaldo," David shouted. "Without you, we would be fighting for relegation!"

"Look at Cristiano, running around with his arms wide open," said Edo. "That's not his usual goal celebration."

"He appears slightly different since he lost his son," said David solemnly.

"True," said Edo. "He even let Bruno Fernandes take a penalty last week against Arsenal. How crazy is that?"

"It's pretty unbelievable," said David, shaking his head. "It's never happened before!"

Edo lowered his head.

"I suppose his perspective on life must have shifted a little," he said.

ONENESS

Tollgate Pub, Manchester
August 2022

◇

Ronaldinho—The Source of Football

The Beauty Beyond Winning and Losing

It was early in the new season, Cristiano Ronaldo's second since returning to Manchester United, who had lost to Brentford 4-0 the previous weekend under the new manager, Erik ten Hag and were now facing Liverpool on a cool Monday evening.

Fans organised a pre-match protest against the Manchester United owners, and they gathered in a Tollgate pub, some half a mile from the Old Trafford stadium.

"Tickets, please," said a lady at the entrance and an oversized guard stuck his giant hand out.

"Tickets?" said Edo, looking confused. "Match tickets?"

"We don't have tickets," said David. "We're just joining the protest. Can't we enter the pub without match tickets?"

"Unfortunately, not," said the lady sternly.

"Oh, come on, let them in," said a guy with the infamous yellow and green scarf identical to the one David wore. "They're with us!"

The lady looked up at the tall guard, who nodded and let Edo and David into the pub.

David was dressed in black with a green and gold scarf, the same as most of the inhabitants of the pub. The traditional colours had belonged to the original Manchester United when they were known as Newton Heath, as David had explained to Edo. Fans adopted the colours as a symbol of opposition to the United owners, the Glazer family.

Edo wore a basic grey hoodie and stood out from the rest of the crowd.

"This is the worst Manchester United in the club's history," said David. "We're bottom of the league. There's no vision, no hope." The barwoman nodded, handing David two pints of cold ale. "Something needs to change from within," he added. "The Glazers need to sell the club and go."

"There's space over in the corner," said Edo, taking a beer from David and shuffling his way across the packed room towards a gap where people were playing pool.

"We've been without a trophy since Mourinho was in charge in 2017," David said as they broke through the lively crowd. "This season will be no different, judging by what we've seen. It's embarrassing. I'm afraid of what's going to happen today. We haven't won a league match against Liverpool in almost five years. It's bad, mate."

"Are we alright here?" Edo asked a group of fans as he spotted two vacant bar stools right by the window.

"It's just bad," David said, putting his pint down and opening a bag of pork scratchings. "Just very bad."

"Cheer up, David," said Edo. "As we discussed, something can only be bad from a certain perspective. What is good for one is bad for another. Therefore, good *inevitably* carries bad within it, and vice versa. One cannot exist without the other in the grand scheme."

"Yes, and *both* are needed for personal and collective growth," David said. "But this club is simply broken! Money dictates *everything* in this club. That's why we have players who can't play serious games. I'm afraid Liverpool will smash us again tonight."

"Why don't you sit down, David?" said Edo, but David shook his head, preferring to stand.

"Ever since this guy left us as manager," he said, pointing grimly toward a black and white picture of Alex Ferguson during his early days in the club. "It's been bad."

"What's been bad for Manchester United fans has been good for Liverpool fans," said Edo, pressing his point. "Therefore, good, and bad are subjective perspectives of the world. The ego creates such subjective perspectives because it can't see other perspectives. Remember, a big ego means low compassion, David. And compassion is about understanding *other* perspectives."

"Well, we have also established that football is a game of egos," said David. "Football is a game of survival. Egos win games, my friend. You have to admire Ronaldo, the only valuable asset of this club at the moment. His determination to win is unique. He's been through so much, and he *still* keeps growing, keeps *rising*."

"Yeah, his ego is huge," said Edo. "There's zero compassion for opponents. There's only the aim to keep adding layers of glory to his ultimate egoic structure *CR7*—the one he identifies with most."

"Let's go outside. There's more space in the garden, and it's quieter," said David.

Edo nodded, following his friend back through the crowd and into a beer garden.

"Well, that's nice," said Edo as they arrived back in the cool air. "Now, David, football might indeed be the game of egos, but many of the game's elements come from a state of mind beyond egoic perspectives when one connects to the world and their true self."

"What do you mean by true self?" said David.

"It's the self that appears when ego doesn't run the show," said Edo. "The true identity shows up when you stop seeking meaning in physical form, thoughts and emotions. Thus, you no longer identify with egoic structures such as *I am Man United* or *I am CR7*."

David looked confused as they sat down at a wooden table. Edo took a large swig of beer and continued.

"Yes, David. In the realm of form, thoughts, and emotions, good can't exist without bad and bad can't exist without good. But sometimes, that very absurd realisation can lead to accepting things as they come. Full acceptance of the situation you happen to be in can lead to a game of the purest beauty beyond the euphoria of winning and the misery of losing—an inner state of consciousness where all living and non-living things merge into one. It's a state of consciousness beyond good and bad, beyond the kingdom of ego—beyond that space where winning and losing matter in terms of evolution. It's *beyond* time. It's a space where good equals bad and where losing equals winning. Only there can one truly understand one's perspective is not the only valuable one. I am talking about the truly *beautiful* game of football, David—the game that is *always* present for everybody who can detach from egoic needs and the game's laws and see them from a distance. Those beings see the world holistically rather than through limited subjective perspectives of good and bad. It's when life becomes complete, and nothing else is to be added or taken away. It is *beyond* survival, David. There's nothing to defend there, nor life or image to enhance."

David sat up and finished chewing on a pork scratching.

"But then it is not football anymore," he said. "Football is about winning and losing, Edo. And didn't we already conclude that life is the same?"

"Ronaldinho!" Edo exclaimed suddenly. "What about Ronaldinho, then?"

"*What about* Ronaldinho?" said David, rinsing his mouth with beer.

"Ronaldinho is *proof* that football doesn't need to be about ego," said Edo. "He is proof that life doesn't need to be about winning and losing."

"Why do you say that?" said David.

Edo stood up for a moment, examining his trousers for dampness from the bench before sitting down and leaning into David.

"Ronaldinho is complete *already*," said Edo. "You can see it by his smile. Whether he wins or loses, it doesn't make a difference. The smile is *always* there from ear to ear. It's only the *game* that matters to him. He's never needed to prove anything. Wherever he played, it was *only* about the pure joy of playing. It was about inspiration, love, creativity, giving and sharing on a level that a person chained to ego can't understand. And it's *certainly* not understandable to Cristiano, whose life is about proving things."

David scrunched up his nose and took another big mouthful of beer.

"Ronaldinho once said that God gives gifts to everyone," Edo continued. "Some can write, some can dance, while Ronaldinho received the skill of playing football."[19]

"*Blessed* is the one who is aware of his gifts," David said, nodding enthusiastically.

"Blessed?" said Edo. "Yeah, call it whatever you like, but it's about connecting to your *true self* because that state of consciousness is a gift in itself. Only when you step beyond your ego can you see the truth—truth beyond subjective perspective. That's when you see who you *really* are. But there's nothing to prove anymore because you are *already* complete. That's where Ronaldinho's creativity comes from."

The United fans formed a circle in the garden and started chanting anti-Liverpool songs. *Have you ever seen Gerrard win the league? Have you ever seen Gerrard win the league?*

"Yeah, but you see, mate," said David. "*That's* why he only lasted a few years, whereas Ronaldo has endured over twenty years winning *five* Ballon d'Ors versus Ronaldinho's *one*."

"It's true," said Edo. "That's what ego *does*. Cristiano is *never* satisfied. He seeks completion through outer objects—individual recognition, trophies and goals. But Ronaldinho is already complete."

"I think Ronaldo is more football than Ronaldinho is," said David. "As we said earlier, football is about winning and sacrifice. It's about evolving through good and bad situations. That's what Ronaldo brings to the table."

"Yes, David, that might be right," said Edo. "But only at the *surface* level of the game. Right now, we're not talking about evolving but rather about one's all-encompassing connectivity to all life forms and the source itself—the source of football. Once you identify with trophies and judge who is better, you lose the beautiful game of football because you abandon your true self. You neglect the beauty beyond winning and losing. That's when football becomes a beautiful game for the winner only and a game of suffering for the loser. Ronaldinho is pure absoluteness, completeness, inspiration."

David nodded, impressed by the depth of Edo's speech, spurred on by the pint before him.

"Okay, think about this, David," said Edo. "It's as if you and Arafat each had a bakery, and you were both happy with what you had. Sometimes, he would sell more bread. Sometimes, you would sell more. It wouldn't matter because you didn't seek meaning in that. And, sure, you *might* still evolve to the point where you can afford an electric dome oven or whatever you might call it and make the magnificent Shepherd's loaf. On the other hand, Arafat might end up with nothing but a wooden rolling pin and a shitty second-hand oven from the last century. But if you were both connected to your true selves, you would be fine with your circumstances. And there would be peace in the street regardless of what you possess. And the funny thing is, David, when you reach that level of consciousness—when you *accept* the current situation *as it is*—that's when you get the most out of it and make unimaginably delicious bread with only your wooden rolling pin and your old oven and your sheer joy of using them."

The United fans' anti-Liverpool chanting grew louder as they consumed more beer. David watched them for a moment, smiling.

"That's the *true* power Cristiano doesn't understand," Edo continued. "It's the power which comes when you are *true*—when you experience your *true* self. I mean, Ronaldinho still wins games, regardless. He just doesn't seek meaning in that. He evolves *differently*."

"I hear what you're saying, Edo," said David. "But have you considered that Ronaldinho simply didn't have the *discipline, will, and consistency* it took to be the best footballer of all? He was more into *nightlife, music and dancing*."

"You're right," Edo said. "He didn't have what it took to be the greatest footballer. The man was football *itself*, in its purest form. Ronaldinho was *life* in its purest form. And as the representation of the purest form of life and football, there was no need to keep proving himself in big clubs because he already had it wherever he went."

"Had what?"

"The game," said Edo. "The joy of playing, David. How else could you explain that goal against Chelsea at Stamford Bridge? He received the ball on the edge of the box. The Chelsea defence held their position, waiting for him to make a move. But he never made that move. Instead, he did a couple of samba dance steps before toe-poking the ball past three defenders, leaving Petr Čech watching open-mouthed as the ball hit the back of the net. Čech didn't move. Nobody moved. They couldn't. It was as if some cosmic force aligned the angles perfectly for the ball not to hit any of those players in front of him. That shot was just different, man."

"It *was* a great goal, I must admit," said David, smiling.

Edo pointed at the sky.

"Let me quote Ronaldinho," he said. "*No matter who you are, the simple things in life lead you to believe you can achieve anything.*"[20]

"But he couldn't achieve anything," said David. "He couldn't stay at Barcelona and win another five Balon d'Ors as Ronaldo did."

"To achieve anything doesn't necessarily mean to win trophies," said Edo. "It means to feel the same level of fulfilment wherever you are, regardless of the fleeting nature of emotions and thoughts, regardless of the score. It's *absoluteness* that can't be embellished or diminished. It's the small things, as Ronaldinho said, that make life worth living—all with that same smile and a sparkle in his eyes—with the same love of the game, for the ball, for his opponents, for the audience and himself. All with the same connectivity to the whole of life. Oneness!"

Deeper Than Loyalty

Can Love Come From Outside?

"Love is the answer!" Edo said as they wandered back into the crowded pub.

"They do say that," said David as they reached a jukebox. He dropped in a couple of coins and selected *I Don't Want To Talk About It* by Rod Stewart.

"Do you love somebody, David?" said Edo.

"Yes," said David. "I love my mother and my brother. I love my girlfriend, and, as you are aware, I love Manchester United."

"Why do you love Manchester United?" said Edo.

"*I don't wanna talk about it—*" David sang along to the song, and the whole pub joined in.

How you broke my heart—

"Why do I love Manchester United?" David said, smiling. "Because, as you can see, mate, I feel part of something bigger when I support Man United—part of a community. Who do you love, Edo?"

Edo thought about it for a moment.

"I think I have affection towards certain people—but when it comes to love," he paused. "I believe love is *everything*. It's all around us all the time. It's the source of everything."

"What do you mean, mate?" said David.

"I believe love comes from within," said Edo. "It's not reserved for a single person, a family, a girlfriend or a club. Love is *everything*. Love *is* football. But it starts within."

"Are you still seeing that girl?" David asked.

"Not anymore. We broke up," said Edo glumly.

"Well, clearly I can understand that," said David, patting his friend on the back and laughing. "Just kidding, mate," he said.

Edo laughed a little and smiled at his friend.

"I guess we weren't destined to be together," he said as he moved his shoulders to the song's beat. "She was *beautiful,* though."

"So you fell in love with her at one point?" said David.

"Well, I thought I did," said Edo. "But I realised if I had to *fall* into something, it couldn't be real, sustainable. If love comes from within and everything comes from love, you can't fall into it. You can only be part of something already absolute and everywhere—that which is for everyone. You can only be a *part* of the game of purest beauty. You can't own it."

"I don't know about that, my friend," said David, moving entirely with the song.

"Love *is* Ronaldinho," Edo said. "*Ronaldinho state of consciousness*. To love everything is to love yourself as well. If you don't love yourself, then you can't love others. If you love yourself, then you love everything! You love life. You *are* life! Even those situations and people that might not appear suitable for you are simply part of the wide picture of love."

"I don't agree," said David. "You can still love others if you don't love yourself."

"But is that real love, then?" said Edo. "Is it the all-encompassing absolute love I am talking about? It can't be, David, because the love I am referring to comes from *within*. It can't come from the outside, not even from the most magnificent person in the world or the most amazing football club. The way you just described love might only be seeking meaning in another person and getting attracted to a person or a club because of the *idea* they give you about *yourself*."

"Yeah? And what's the problem with that? That's the point!" said David, sinking the last of his drink.

"I'll tell you the problem," said Edo. "The *problem* occurs when you seek too much meaning from a certain person, or when that person can no longer give you the picture of yourself they used to give you. That's when you start seeing the person differently. So-called *love* starts falling apart. Because it was not *real* love in the first place but only an idea of what love should be. You can't explain true love, and you can't find it in the physical form."

"Don't kill the love, man," said David.

"On the other hand," said Edo. "Loving yourself means accepting yourself. Loving yourself means *you have already found meaning* and don't need to seek it externally. At that point, you can provide all the love to other people because you have connected to the true *source* of love."

"And to your true self?" said David.

"And to your true self as well, correct," said Edo.

"So you didn't love yourself, and that's why you broke up with your girlfriend?" said David.

Edo thought about it for a moment.

"That's a good question," he said. "Even though I *thought* I loved myself, I was still seeking a piece of the puzzle from her. Or maybe there was a part of me that I didn't love."

"What about *my* love for Manchester United, then?" said David. "Does that mean I need to love myself to love Manchester United?"

Edo smiled and put his hand on his friend's shoulder.

"It's about seeking love through identification with objects and believing the community would give you meaning," he said. "But as I said, man, when you love yourself, then you love the whole of life—the whole of football. You don't need to identify with a person or a club to love and be loved. And *that's* when your compassion grows—your view widens, and love becomes your power source."

"Sounds nice," said David. "But I see love as a decision. Loyalty! That's what love is about! I see my love towards my girlfriend as a decision to strive through our ups and downs, just as I keep supporting Manchester United through their ups and downs, the same way Ferguson thrived in Manchester United through theirs, learning along the way to finally create a perfect system."

"Fans seek so much meaning in their clubs," said Edo. "When their club wins, they are happy. When the club loses, they become sad."

"Exactly," said David. "That's when the *real* fans show up—when their club loses! And those so-called fans who can't—or don't want to—deal with losses prove they have no value to the club and soon lose interest. *That's* why love is a decision!"

"Very good, David," said Edo. "Love is great any way you feel it, I guess! And I relate to what you are saying. But a deeper dimension of love dwells here all the time, and no one can take it away. The difference is—is it in the name of *love* or *love for something?*"

The whole pub crowd kept singing through the third chorus.

I don't wanna talk about it—how you broke my heart.

"Take, for example, Paul Scholes, Ryan Giggs or Gary Neville," said David. "They stayed at United for their whole careers. That's love! Or Francesco Totti—*Il Principe!* He was my favourite non-United player. Real Madrid offered to buy him at one point in his career. He had the opportunity to join the mighty *Galácticos* and play alongside Zidane, Beckham, Figo, Ronaldo, and Owen. But he refused because he wanted to stay at his beloved Roma. Totti is a football Romeo, Edo! Totti wouldn't have stayed in Roma if he hadn't truly loved himself. As you said, he didn't need to seek meaning anywhere else. Because he understood love comes from within—one's home club. And yet, he was the hero of the fans. Otherwise, he would have gone where the money was."

Edo thought about it.

"Or," he said. "Maybe he was seeking meaning by identifying with Roma?"

"Ronaldinho was never loyal to any of the numerous clubs he played for," barked David. "He didn't *love* them."

"Okay, so he didn't love certain clubs like Totti loved Roma," said Edo. "But that's the path he chose to follow."

"The path of never-ending chase?" said David, glancing over the crowd between him and the bar.

"Rather, a path of spreading love wherever he goes," said Edo.

"Well, Totti spread love in his club," David said, shuffling forward. "He didn't need to go anywhere to love and be loved. Totti *is* Rome. All the knowledge he got was from one club, one environment. Roma is something that *defines* Totti. It defines who he is. Totti *is* Rome."

"Yes, we agree on that one," said Edo.

"Ronaldinho will *never* have an army of loyal fans behind him," said David. "He will never be crowned a prince like Totti, whose city of Rome shines on him for eternity. Totti *is* Rome!"

"Yes, well, Ronaldinho is *everything*," said Edo.

"Totti is a loyal prince."

"Ronaldinho is everything. And *nothing*. At the same time."

"Totti will die in the Colosseum."

"Ronaldinho will die free—only with the ball by his side."

"Totti is *the one*."

"Ronaldinho is *one*."

"Life is about loyalty," said David as he began to push his way through the crowd to the bar. "Totti's farewell to football was something else, Edo. Seventy thousand fans cried at the Stadio Olimpico while their prince made his final speech. Men, women, players, coaches, presidents, and staff were all brokenhearted and in tears because Totti was retiring. That's some love right there, my friend. Totti gave himself to the fans that day completely. It was his love letter to them. He assured them that he was only theirs. I remember the content of the letter to the word."

David stopped mid-crowd and began quoting as if reading an imaginary letter.

"*Today, time has come to tap me on the shoulder and tell me it's time to grow up. As of tomorrow, you'll be an adult. Take off those shorts and boots because, starting today, you are a man.*

You can no longer enjoy the smell of the grass, the sun on your face, as you bear down on the opponent's goal with the adrenaline consuming you and the joy of celebrating. Over the past few months, I've asked myself why I'm waking up from this dream. Imagine you are a child having a nice dream, and your mother wakes you up to go to school. You want to keep dreaming and try to slip back into the dream but never can. This time, it's not a dream but a reality, I'm afraid."[21]

"That's moving," said Edo. "But you see, Ronaldinho is football itself, and no one could ever awaken him from what he *is*."

From Hooliganism to Equality

When Identification With the Badge Is Complete

"Enough is enough," David said, changing his mind about another beer and heading for the exit. "Let's sing some songs instead and make the Glazers leave!"

Edo followed David out of the pub, where a group of fans had got off a tram at the Trafford Bar station and were blocking the traffic and making their way up to Old Trafford.

A group of ten Liverpool fans were nervously moving in the opposite direction, closely guarded by police. A couple of the United fans tried to reach the Liverpool fans, but the police stopped them.

The United fans sang loudly, and someone threw a flare among the Liverpool fans.

Build a bonfire, build a bonfire. Put the Scousers on the top. Put the City in the middle and burn the fucking lot.

More police joined the scene to protect the Liverpool fans, and the United fans sang even more aggressively.

United! United! United!

"You see, David," said Edo as the pair tried to escape the action. "Identification inevitably creates suffering."

"But these guys are simply hooligans," David said.

"Well, that's how society perceives them," said Edo. "It's just the way we see them. But in reality, they are just people who are more identified with their club than you are, David."

"Excuse me!" said David. "No one loves United as much as me, thanks very much. *United! United! United!*"

"What about these guys who are ready to fight another group of fans in the name of Manchester United?" said Edo. "Don't they love the club more than you? They *believe* they are better than others through their identification with the badge. They completely identify and, as such, are led far from their true selves. They identify so much that they are ready to kill for the badge."

David turned his head back to watch where the United fans were still shouting at the Liverpool fans.

"Do you believe you are better than Liverpool fans, David?" said Edo.

"Of course I do," said David awkwardly. "Liverpool are shit!"

"You see, that's my point," said Edo. "As I said, identification *inevitably* creates suffering. The identification of hooligans is a *total* identification. They not only create suffering for themselves but also for others—and all in the name of the badge. And, sure, some are in it for the adrenaline, the fun or because they are fighting something deeper inside themselves. There are also those with a strong rush of testosterone fever. But their identification with the club is what they all use to channel that."

David turned around again, and the pair reached a safe distance from the trouble behind a group of hundreds of fans chanting loudly.

We want Glazers out, say we want Glazers out.

“I’ll tell you why identification is important, Edo,” said David. “Without strong identification, we would have the Super League by now.”

“What do you mean?” said Edo.

David cleared his throat and spat on the ground.

“As you know, Edo,” he said. “In April last year, twelve of the biggest European clubs decided to break away from the rest of the European competitions and form a new closed-format league. Football was a moment from changing forever. And if you remember, the driving force against the Super League was the fans. We got out in the streets and said *no* to the Super League.”

“Well, yes, I know all that,” said Edo.

“Okay, good,” said David. “But do you know why we said no to the Super League? It was because we identified with our clubs so much and didn’t want to lose what we had. We didn’t want to lose our relationship with football or our feeling of togetherness when we went to games—the misery of losing and the euphoria of winning. We didn’t want to lose small clubs or the romance that football brings. We didn’t want to lose the communities that exist only because of football. Football and communities mutually support each other, Edo. We didn’t want to lose the lower leagues that would end up without money. We didn’t want to lose football as we know it.”

“Yeah,” Edo said soberly. “I hear you, man.”

“And yes, ultimately, we didn’t want to lose rivalry between clubs,” said David. “I didn’t want to lose our rivalry with Liverpool, which is deeply entrenched in who we are as Man United fans and goes way beyond the football world, back to the industrial revolution. Did you know that they built the Manchester Ship Canal to bypass the port of Liverpool, bringing raw material directly to the Manchester mills? And the rivalry goes back even *further* than that, Edo. Football only exaggerated the whole thing. God forbid we lose the rivalry now as we have twenty championship titles and Liverpool have nineteen."

"Yeah, your enemy strengthens your identity," said Edo, listening intently with his hands in his pockets.

"Strong identification was why the Super League didn't happen," said David. "And if there weren't people out on the streets, shouting *We are Man Utd, We are Chelsea,* or *We are Arsenal,* those greedy bastards would have broken away and formed the Super League."

"Yes, ego protected itself," said Edo. "Collective ego protected itself. It was afraid of losing the part of its identity which makes it what it is perceived to be."

More fans joined their group from another street, and now, more than a thousand of them blocked the roads, chanting loudly.

"You need to understand," David continued. "There was *so* much at stake, Edo. Do you know how important English football clubs are to their local communities? They conduct health, sports, education and many other projects. All that was at stake with the Super League."

"How come?" said Edo, enjoying David's deep knowledge of the subject.

"Because, my friend," said David. "The top six clubs—those whose owners agreed on forming the Super League before they finally abolished the project—earn so much money from television rights that they sustain the entire English football pyramid, down to the lower leagues. In return, the lower leagues serve as a talent pool from where the top clubs draw players. Without the money lower league clubs get from the top of the pyramid, clubs from the third or fourth division would rely only on gates and sponsorship money. And I'm sure you know, mate, that we are living through tough times. There isn't much money for the poor, I'm afraid. Money is reserved for the rich."

Edo thought for a moment.

"Ok, David. So how can you still support Man United when the owners, the Glazer family, were among the founding members of the Super League?"

"Because the Glazers are not Man United," said David. "Not after that! They are my *enemy*."

"They weren't your enemy when they brought Cristiano, Van Persie, Vidić and others, though," said Edo.

"Correct," said David. "They *weren't*. But they are *now*."

"Okay," said Edo. "But the moment they started buying players for a hundred million pounds a piece was when you *should* have said they were your enemy. The Super League project didn't appear overnight, man. The game has been heading toward elitism for decades."

"True," said David. "But we couldn't *know* where it was heading. How can we know the future? Man, the Super League would mean the *end* of football as we know it—no rivalry, no passion and no World Cup either. FIFA threatened to *expel participating* players from the World Cup."

A few thousand fans now approached Old Trafford chanting louder and more aggressively than ever.

He's gonna die, he's gonna die, Joel Glazer's gonna die.

How we kill him, I don't know, cut him up from head to toe.

All I know is Glazer's gonna die.

The police wall separated more Liverpool fans. Still, despite the protection, United fans threw a couple of flares into the Liverpool crowd again while a group of United fans with a *Red Army* flag smashed into the police wall, trying to break it down.

"Red Army!" David shouted before lowering his voice. "Back in the day of the peak English hooliganism, the Red Army were the biggest football hooligan firm in the country," he said. "Cities across England were terrified when Manchester United fans visited. But those same people, some of the most fanatic fans, have done great things for the local community through the years."

The chanting of the fans had become almost deafening.

Red Army! Red Army! Red Army!

"Answer me this, Edo," said David, raising his voice. "How do you explain that football has become the world's biggest platform for equality if the essence of football is based on identifying with the badge and making enemies of people who support a different badge? Support for minorities is often expressed at stadiums where fans simultaneously beat each other for having a different membership card."

"True," said Edo. "Football is, weirdly, both a xenophobic and supportive environment."

"It is," said David. "But is football only supporting equality to cover up its past of violence, racism, and corruption?"

Edo shrugged.

"You can see it that way," he said.

"And what's another way of seeing it?" said David.

Edo thought about it before speaking.

"In the grand scheme of things, strong identification tends to create intense suffering and separate us from our true selves so drastically that our soul will revolt and dissolve all those layers of identification, setting us free. We might get to the point where we ask ourselves, what does it mean that I am white, black, straight, gay? Or Liverpool or United, or a baker?

"Or a CR7?" said David.

"Exactly," said Edo. "Strong identification with any of those can create so much suffering that sometimes concepts of who is bigger, stronger, or better simply dissolve, and we become liberated."

"And what happens then?" said David.

"What happens, David, is that compassion arises," said Edo. "Empathy arises along with the idea of equality. What happens is that football becomes *a* supportive environment. What happens is we become free like Ronaldinho."

The Manchester United fans gathered before the stadium to protest against the club's owners and thousands joined them as they entered the stadium for the match.

David and Edo moved away from the crowd to make space for the people with tickets.

"It was always about football for Ronaldinho," said Edo, watching the crowd pour into the ground. "It was never about the club's badge nor some big achievements. That's why his game was *absolute.* In Grêmio, Brazil, where he started—and later in Paris, it was *always* the same—*pure* football, *pure* joy. Then he transferred to Barcelona, and the game of football changed forever. Ronaldinho added a new dimension to the game—the *Ronaldinho* dimension. We had never seen anything like it. His first game at Camp Nou unveiled everything Barcelona fans needed to know about the new magician in town. The goal he scored against Sevilla on his home debut was *poetry.*"

"Yes!" said David excitedly. "It's crazy that it was his first goal for Barcelona!"

"Absolutely," said Edo. "Ronaldinho received the ball in his own half, took on one player, then nutmegged another before freeing himself in space for a shot. And what a shot it was! He struck the ball from maybe thirty meters as hard as possible, and it went in off the crossbar. It was the most delicious way to present himself to the Barca home fans."

"Yep," said David, laughing with joy. "Frank Rijkaard grabbed his head as if he couldn't believe what kind of player he'd brought to the club."

"That's right," said Edo. "It was as if he knew he had brought in a player who would soon receive the *Ballon d'Or*."

Edo paused briefly to glance at the United Trinity sculpture, made in honour of the Manchester United legends.

"Ronaldinho became immortal," he continued. "Two seasons later, he dragged Barcelona to the final of the Champions League in Paris, where they beat Arsenal in an epic showdown."

"What a game," said David.

"He was crowned the best player in the world," said Edo. "But essentially, nothing changed. He was absolute."

"Wouldn't he be more absolute if he stayed in Barcelona and won five more Ballon d'Ors?" said David.

Edo shook his head.

"That's the thing, David," he said. "Ronaldinho didn't *need* to stay in Barca and prove anything to anybody. His game was proof in itself beyond any rational understanding. Later, he went to Milan, back to Brazil in Flamengo and Atlético Mineiro, and then to Mexico, where he played for Querétaro. *Wherever* he played, it was all about playing the game's purest form. Ronaldinho didn't have colours, and he didn't have enemies. He didn't identify with the badge. He wasn't Barcelona, nor Milan or Flamengo."

"Yeah, and that's why he couldn't fit into many teams," David said. "After all, some of the greatest managers couldn't find him a place in the squad."

"For God's sake," Edo said. "Even when he ended up imprisoned in a Paraguayan prison after entering the country with a fake passport, *nothing* changed. With the same passion he was nutmegging Gennaro Gattuso and Sergio Ramos fifteen years earlier, he was now nutmegging serial killers in the prison courtyard with the same smile on his face and the same no-look pass on his boot. As I said, he *is* football."

"Why would he fake passports?" said David. "And why would he have unpaid taxes and swing guns around in pictures *if* he was so pure as you claim?"

"I don't know," said Edo. "Even the *purest* ones do crazy shit, David. But that smile he brings with him transcends all those crazy things, shining a new light on them. Life puts you in unexpected situations and makes you do unexpected things. But when you do crazy shit with love, it's different. According to reports, Ronaldinho was in good spirits despite being jailed.[22] So he could share his energy with his cell mates who needed positivity and love."

"Why would they need love?" said David. "They're in prison for a reason!"

"Yes, they are there for a reason," said Edo. "And the *essential* reason is because they lack love or carry some profound trauma. You can only hurt others if you are hurt yourself, man."

"Are you sure about that?" said David.

Edo looked up at the sky and then back to the crowd.

"Ronaldinho was there to give love, David," said Edo. "He was there to share smiles, show them love, and help them love themselves, as Ronaldinho loves himself—football—life. I mean, still, he wiped the floor with them, let's take nothing away from that. Apparently, he scored five goals and assisted six in an 11-2 victory for his side—all with the same smile."

"The same smile eh?" said David.

"Yep," said Edo. "That's what genuine freedom *is*. Outside needs and wants do not drive it. It is driven by realising you are already complete, and by simply playing the game of football. It's when you can rely on your intuition and the higher intelligence which is so different to the basic intelligence the mind uses."

"What if he was simply more talented than others?" said David. "What about that, my friend?"

"Well, that's difficult to deny," said Edo. "But Ronaldinho explained quite nicely that his game was based on improvisation because, as a forward, he didn't have time to overthink. *You have a second, rarely more, to decide whether to dribble, shoot, or pass to the right or left. It is instinct that gives the orders*."[23]

"*How* can that kind of freedom be achieved?" David asked.

"By not identifying with form," said Edo. "By not believing you are Barcelona, you are the Ballon d'Or winner or the prisoner—by not believing you are the best, *or* the worst. They're all physical forms and thoughts for the ego to attach to and make part of your identity. But those are just ideas—*mind-created* concepts. Yes, he *is* all of that, but on the *surface* only. Essentially, he is free of those mind-created concepts. And if something is mind-created, we are again in the egoic realm where good doesn't exist without bad. Whenever you identify with something, that something inevitably creates suffering."

David stood wide-eyed, looking at the crowd.

"So you claim Ronaldinho didn't suffer in prison?" he said.

"Look, David," said Edo. "Ronaldinho's state of consciousness is beyond good and bad, which can liberate you even if you are behind bars. True peace is the result of that state of consciousness."

"But he was still the prisoner. You can't deny that fact."

"No, he was *in* the prison. He wasn't *the* prisoner. Just as he was *playing* for Barcelona. He wasn't Barcelona. Just as he won the title of *best player in the world.* He was not *the* best player in the world. His mind was free from identification, and therefore he was free."

"How can somebody not suffer while in prison?" David said. "I don't think that's possible, Edo."

"It's possible if you see it for what it is rather than identifying with the situation," Edo said. "And more importantly, if you don't identify with your *thoughts* about a certain situation—that's the challenging part."

"What thoughts?" said David.

"Well," said Edo. "I'm talking about the thoughts that arise when you are in a difficult situation. For instance, thoughts that say things like *I am screwed.* If you identify with those thoughts, then you *become* those thoughts. You become *screwed.* The key is to recognise thoughts as they arise. That's when they lose their power over you. The same applies to the emotions created by those thoughts."

"What emotions?" said David.

Edo found an old chewing gum wrapper in his pocket and toyed with it while still staring at the crowds from a distance.

"Emotions of anxiety, stress, depression and so on," he said. "If you can recognise them as they arise, the de-identification process begins, David. And you don't *become* those emotions.

They lose their power over you. You are still *absolute* Ronaldinho despite dark clouds in your inner sky. But once they dissipate, the sun is still there, shining. Ronaldinho's smile is still shining, regardless of loss or victory!"

"Right," said David, smiling at the sky.

Edo paused momentarily, listening to the chants get quieter as the fans moved inside Old Trafford. Finally, he spoke.

"That's what makes you free even amid the most horrific terror or, in what you might see as the most horrible situation," he said. "Ultimately, Ronaldinho wasn't even a prisoner. He just *was*. And he happened to be in prison."

"So what's the point you are trying to make?" said David curiously. "To accept any situation as it is?"

"That's another way of saying it," said Edo. "To accept any situation *as it is*—to let it be. That's what freedom *is.*"

Smoke from a nearby flare surrounded them, and Edo coughed a little.

"But the main thing is," he said through his coughs. "You need to *accept* your *thoughts* about the situation. Thoughts make a situation good or bad, David. When you accept your thoughts, the moment they arise, you distance yourself from them. You see them clearly, and you step out of the realm of good and bad. You step into the realm of *Ronaldinho*. And suddenly, it's *alright*."

"Don't you think that's a way of giving in and becoming indifferent to life?" said David.

"Ego *mistakes* indifference for acceptance," said Edo. "There's a completely different energy about acceptance. Acceptance shows you the way, while indifference makes you numb. Only when you accept the situation as it is—only in that state of mind—can true and profound changes occur—the kind of change that starts from within."

Art—Where Good Equals Bad

Expression of True Self

Kick-off approached, and the remaining fans with tickets started filling the stadium. The protest slowly ended with only the most dedicated fans holding the posters with anti-Glazers messages.

Edo and David observed pictures on the wall in front of the stadium depicting Manchester United's most famous historical moments.

"Wow, what astonishing pictures!" said David.

"I like this one," said Edo, pointing at a picture of Cristiano Ronaldo scoring a famous free kick against Portsmouth. "Look at the wall of Portsmouth defenders. They're shitting themselves, pal. And Cristiano's face—look—a man ready to kill!"

"And kill them he did!" said David. "What a strike that was—one of the best free kicks I've ever seen. The trajectory of that ball broke the laws of physics."

"They're such splendid pictures!" said Edo. "They were shot at the perfect moment. It's *art*!"

David nodded.

"You see, David," said Edo. "Art comes from *Ronaldinho's* consciousness. *Art is beyond* the law of good and bad. It comes from a state of mind where good *equals* bad. I'm talking about the *real* art here."

"Art?" said David. "As in painting? Like photography? Music?"

"Yes," said Edo. "As in painting, photography, and music. And including writing, sculpture, dance and film—pretty much everything—baking bread, for instance, and football, man."

"Football?" said David, his eyes lighting up.

"Football," said Edo.

David thought for a moment.

"But football is *life*, not art!" he said, becoming annoyed. "Didn't we already reach that conclusion, Edo? Football is life with some *elements* of art."

"Some people believe football is entirely art, David," said Edo.

"And who are those people?" said David, bending down to tie his shoelace.

"Massimiliano Allegri," said Edo.

"Massimiliano?" said David, who had a deep knowledge of Serie A in Italy. "He won six Scudettos as a coach—five with Juventus and one with Milan. Amazing! He was supposed to succeed Ole as United manager, but we got Ralf Rangnick instead."

David stood up and jogged to catch up with Edo.

"Aren't *we* lucky?" he said sarcastically.

Edo looked at the ground to check *his* shoelaces.

"You know, after Allegri left Juventus, someone asked him to reveal his secret of successful managing," Edo said. "Allegri said that in Italy *all* tactics are bullshit and that football should be seen as *art*—something like that, anyway. *World-class players are world-class artists*, he said."[24]

"Did he really say that?" said David.

"Yes," said Edo. "From memory, he said he didn't have to teach them anything but just let them play and give them freedom."

"Freedom?" said David, screwing up his nose.

"Yeah, and he got that one right," said Edo. "Art and freedom arrive together. There has to be *freedom*—from identification—for *true* art to emerge. *And once an artist finds freedom, the rest is up to them*, Allegri claimed. He said the coach is just a spectator watching a show by the artists."

"Well, he certainly coached some of the best!" said David. "Fat Ronaldo, Ibrahimović, Dybala, Pirlo—"

"Ronaldinho!" shouted Edo.

"Ronaldinho?" David said suspiciously. "I don't think they got along that well, my friend. Apparently, they clashed over Ronaldinho's late nights out."

"Okay," said Edo solemnly.

"Which makes me think that Ronaldinho didn't have the discipline to maintain his football focus," said David. "Maybe he changed clubs a lot because he was a *rebel*. Guardiola made him leave Barcelona. Allegri made him leave Milan."

"Ronaldinho once wrote that he simply plays free and with joy," said Edo. "*I just hear the music*, he said, despite being aware that it was something many coaches didn't understand. *But when I am on the pitch, I will never calculate. Everything will come naturally. Before I have time to think, my feet have already made a decision.*"[25]

"Wow," said David. "So it *is* true. He can really hear the music."

"There's always something rebellious in artists," Edo said. "Something doesn't let artists submit to the established structures. That's the *freedom* I spoke about. If art comes from the level of consciousness free of identification with a club's culture, badge or colours, then surely, he would have been perceived as a rebel by those who identify strongly with those structures."

"Makes sense, I suppose," said David.

"Put it this way," said Edo. "Imagine your bakery makes artistic sourdough bread with corn and mushrooms and God-knows-what while breaking all the traditional rules of sourdough. Following the rules, you can only create what someone had created before. If you are part of the system, you can't fully express your art—your true self. And sure, that bakery might not make enormous profits, but every slice of bread would be unique. Arafat might take most of the customers, but you would be happy with your art and undisturbed by his business. Your bakery would be *the* bakery—not aligned with any rules. Freedom! True art finds the way, David."

David got lost in thought for a second. He stopped and leaned against a post.

"If Allegri couldn't recognise that," Edo continued. "Then the man didn't know what he was talking about when he mentioned that artists need freedom—he didn't understand art. So he didn't deserve to be a witness to the pure art of Ronaldinho either."

"Yeah," said David. "Plus, his theory that football is art doesn't make sense either. Even if we agree that world-class players are artists, what about the other players who are *not*? What about the builders, fighters, friends, neurotics; the lazy ones, loyal ones, stubborn ones; the cheaters, role models, fakers, wise ones, philosophers, winners, and losers?"

"Exactly, my dear friend," said Edo. "Football is life with some aspects of art, rather than art itself."

"Good and bad," David said randomly.

"What about it?" said Edo.

"You said art is not about that," said David.

"Yes," said Edo. "Art is *beyond* that law—no winning and losing—no lessons to learn. Art is *all* there is, David. There's no good or bad art. It exists in both poles equally. And yeah, Ronaldinho might have been a *rebel*, but he was also genuinely interested in dancing and making music. I reckon the music drove him rather than the parties themselves. He said that he never imagined doing anything other than football, but if he thought about it coldly, if he hadn't been a footballer, he would have been a musician."

David nodded and mumbled his agreement as he crouched against the post, resting his legs.

"Ronaldinho is simply an expression of art," said Edo, standing before his friend and waving his hands around. "Whether Ronaldinho is winning or losing, he *always* has that same smile, ready to unleash his magic spell. It's just art—pure art, David. It's pure football *beyond* the fundamental laws of football."

"Ronaldinho was unique. There's no doubt about it," said David.

"Yes," said Edo. "But he was unique because he drew inspiration from his true self." Edo leaned towards David. "And I don't need to remind you of his skills, pal. Ronaldinho could juggle an orange, a gum ball or a chestnut with those magic feet. He could juggle blindfolded or seated. He could assist with his back and dance the samba before taking a shot. He could carry the ball on his lips and give a no-look pass after dribbling past three players. He could do a passing session with a crossbar."

"Mad skills!" said David, smiling and looking into the sky.

"Mad," said Edo. "And Ronaldinho said that he left Milan because Allegri didn't allow him to express himself, which makes me even more certain that Allegri didn't know about true artists."[26]

"Yeah," said David. "But Allegri is still a serial winner."

Edo put his hands in his pockets and swung his leg around.

"The legendary Brazilian midfielder Sócrates reflected on Ronaldinho's first two years in Barcelona," said Edo. "He said that Barca treated Ronaldinho like a king, which is everything an artist could wish for. *It's like getting on the stage, and the whole audience is focused on you while you sing your songs without even opening your mouth. Every song—that's the best feeling in the world,* Sócrates said."

"He was singing his song, there's no doubt about it," said David.

"But I'm not sure if he was the *king*," Edo said. "I believe he simply *was*."

"Was?" said David.

Edo paused, taking a breath.

"Do you remember his famous game against Real Madrid at Santiago *Bernabéu* in 2005?" Edo finally said.

"I do!" said David, sitting up. "Of course I do."

"Every touch of Ronaldinho's was magic," said Edo. "He was *miraculous* whenever he touched the ball—first touch, dribbling, no-look passes. A couple of times, he made Sergio Ramos look stupid. Once or twice, he left Ramos on the deck quite brutally. And sure, Ramos was very young back then, but I don't think he was ever humbled like that again. Ronaldinho showed *no* mercy. Ronaldinho started his run toward the goal from the centre of the pitch, and Ramos went for the tackle instead of covering the space."

"What a novice move!" said David, laughing. "Sergio went for glory, and Dinho taught him a lesson."

"I think that tackle was Ramos panicking," said Edo. "And Ronaldinho simply dribbled past, leaving Ramos on the ground before entering the Real box where Iván Helguera and Iker Casillas were shitting themselves as well. Ronaldinho left them standing and put the ball in the net. Then, the situation was similar for the other Ronaldinho goal, but this time, Ramos changed tactics and decided to cover the space instead. Maybe he would have been better off trying another tackle because Ronaldinho dribbled past him again."

"Ronaldinho was awarded for his magic that night," said David. "Even by Real Madrid supporters. Do you remember, Edo? He received a standing ovation from those Madrid fans—something only Maradona had experienced before him at Santiago *Bernabéu*, and Iniesta after."

"You see, that's proof!" Edo exclaimed. "They applauded the act of *art*. It didn't matter on whose side the art happened. It was just art with no winning and losing—with no good or bad for anybody. Everyone had just experienced *true* art."

David stood up, and the pair slowly made their way home from the great stadium.

"I just want to say," said Edo. "If football *were* a show for Allegri—if it *were* a work of art, then he wouldn't have minded if his team won or lost. There's *no* good and bad in art. It's just a show, as we established, David."

"This play of Man United is a proper tragedy," David said. "I don't even care that we don't have tickets for the match. I'm not paying to watch this tragedy. Even if it's the best show in the world."

"In The Theatre of Dreams," Edo said, glancing at the clock permanently frozen at four minutes past three on February 6th, 1958, when twenty-three people, including eight players of famous Busby Babes United team, died in a plane crash. "This stadium has seen all types of tragedies."

"It has," said David, bowing his head.

"Sometimes, however, football is a comedy!" Edo said, walking in the opposite direction.

"Yep, sometimes it's a joke," said David. "And not a funny one either—the joke so bad that it suffocates the game."

"Suffocates the game?" said Edo, surprised by his friend's words. "What suffocates the game, man?"

"Diving! Faking fouls and injuries!" said David. "That's proper acting. A proper show!"

"True," said Edo. "It can be funny, though. You can see it as a comedy."

"It's bullshit!" said David, raising his voice suddenly. "I had a proper fight with football at one point in my life because of it, Edo."

"Because of diving?" said Edo.

"Yes, *exactly* because of that," said David, irritated. "At the beginning of the 2010s, there was a period when diving became a huge trend! Footballers were diving and faking *all* the time. It was unbearable. It was a proper show! I call them *the peak diving years*."

"I do remember some famous dives from that era," said Edo, smiling.

"Give me one, my friend!" shouted David. "Piss me off!"

"Okay," said Edo. "Do you remember the epic semi-final clashes between Barcelona and Inter in 2010?"

"Do I *remember*?" David laughed. "*Of course*, I remember, mate. You are talking about that *nasty* dive by Sergio Busquets in the second leg in Barcelona. He faked that he was hit in the head by Thiago Motta. He covered his face with his hands, and while he was rolling on the floor, he even moved his hand from his face for a second to check if his trickery had worked out. The camera caught him doing it! Disgraceful! Thiago Motta was awarded a second yellow card and sent off!"

"I don't think I've ever seen you this angry," said Edo, laughing.

"The great Mourinho's Inter managed to lose just 1-0, though," said David. "That was, due to Inter's big win in the first leg, just enough for them to make the final, where they *easily* beat

Bayern 2-0 at Santiago *Bernabéu*. Mourinho reached the peak of his career and earned himself a transfer to Real Madrid."

"What a year they had!" said Edo. "Wesley Sneijder should have been awarded Balon d'Or that year!"

"Agreed!" said David. "But still—*fucking* Sergio Busquets!"

"Great player, though," said Edo.

"He's miserable," said David, kicking an old cigarette box onto the pavement.

"*You watch the game, you don't see Busquets. You watch Busquets, you see the whole game*," Edo said, quoting the ex-Spanish manager Vicente del Bosque.[27] "And, if I may add, if you watch the show, you see a comedy."

"He's still a *faker*!" said David. "I stopped watching football at one point because of him and the other divers. It was 2013, and I said to myself enough was enough. I boycotted the FIFA Confederations Cup that summer because I was so annoyed."

"I see. You were annoyed, David," said Edo.

"Yes, by football."

"Meaning you were annoyed by life!"

"Yes! I was annoyed by life," said David. "Luckily, since they introduced VAR, players can't just fake fouls and get away with it all the time."

"Oh, now you *like* the technology?" said Edo.

David looked at Edo and, for a moment, lost his words.

"You see, David," said Edo. "There are *good* and *bad* sides of the technology. Just as there is with everything that is a part of evolution."

"Right," said David, pausing for thought.

"How did you return to football after that *peak diving* year?" Edo asked.

"Ah," said David. "It wasn't a *huge* fight between football and me. It was more about expressing my feelings. We both knew we would get back together soon."

"Ahh, a true *love* story!" said Edo. "And all the drama that comes along with it."

"Yes, drama," said David. "But drama which made us *stronger*!"

Edo laughed as the football shouts faded into the distance.

"It was the summer before the World Cup in Brazil," said David. "I had to show that I was serious regarding the diving issue before the World Cup summer arrived."

"So you just made a show of it?" said Edo.

"Just a show, my friend, just a show," said David, putting a hand on his friend's shoulder.

"It could have been a comedy play instead," said Edo. "If only you accepted it as it was."

"I couldn't accept that life," said David. "I just couldn't. It *hurt* me."

"That's a shame, David," said Edo. "Because acceptance is an art in itself. If you accept things as they are, you change your perspective. And then you can see art even in things that annoy you. Then, they seem less annoying. You see them as part of the play. You become *part* of the play. It could be a comedy if you *decided* it was a comedy. You are free if you can laugh at things that annoy you."

"It's difficult to laugh sometimes," said David. "I'm no joker, mate."

“Why not?” said Edo. “Some players made it easier for us to recognise their jester roles and not get annoyed. For instance—*Pippo Inzaghi*. That guy was a pure show—diving, comedy, tragedy, spectacle. And it was impossible to get annoyed by him. Pippo must have been the reason Allegri started thinking about art.”

“Pippo? Seriously?” said David.

“Yes, pal,” said Edo. “Only Pippo was able to score two goals in the Champions League final with only one effort on goal and get AC Milan the title.”

“Man, that was an annoying but epic match,” said David. “For Milan, it was proper revenge for the pain Liverpool inflicted on them two years earlier in Istanbul. It was nice to see Liverpool lose the final.”

“Pippo was simply Pippo that night when Andrea Pirlo’s free-kick deflected off Pippo’s shoulder into the net,” said Edo.

“Yes, but he claimed that goal as his own,” said David. “Which he *clearly* didn’t score deliberately. What a drama!”

“Well, we could debate about that,” said Edo. “I’m confident Pippo knew what he was doing when he put himself into that space where the ball was heading.”

“Oh, come on, Edo!” said David. “Don’t be delusional. Pippo is so clumsy.”

“*Or* maybe he wasn’t thinking about it at all,” said Edo. “But rather was moved by his *predatorial* instincts. That made Pippo one of the most feared strikers to ever walk on the earth, despite his clumsy appearance.”

“I’m not sure about that, Edo,” said David. “That second goal wasn’t the slickest either. He barely got anything on that shot.”

“He got just enough for the ball to squeeze below Pepe Reina,” said Edo. “If he’d got more on that ball, Reina might have saved it. That's what makes Pippo great—his vulnerability—which people can sometimes perceive as weakness. On one occasion, Carlo Ancelotti, Allegri’s predecessor at Milan, said that Pippo was not the fastest, strongest, or best jumper. Still, in the box, he was the best striker Ancelotti had ever managed.”[28]

David shook his head at the statement.

“That’s a huge thing to say because Ancelotti coached some of the best players in history,” he said.

“Exactly,” said Edo. “Pippo had something *special*. Yes, he annoyed many with his attitude, but if you could only see him as an actor in the great play of life, without letting your emotions influence the play, you could enjoy him as a pure comedian and laugh.”

David laughed shyly.

“And that’s what Ronaldinho’s smile symbolises, too, David,” Edo said. “It symbolises eternal comedy, laughing regardless of wins or losses, to the divers and fakers; to fighters, friends, neurotics, the lazy ones, the loyal ones, the stubborn ones; to the cheaters, role models, punks, wise ones and the philosophers. Ronaldinho saw it all as part of creation. And that made him—Ronaldinho—a creator himself.”

DEATH

Old Trafford, Manchester

October 2022

◇

Red Card—A Ticket to Heaven

Liberated by the Referee

Autumn arrived in Manchester. It wasn't a light autumn with leaves falling off trees, but a heavy autumn where the leaves had already fallen. The scent of winter was in the air, and the nights were cold.

After suffering initial defeats, Erik ten Hag had managed to regroup his players and catch fifth place in the Premier League when Tottenham visited Old Trafford.

A couple of weeks earlier, and for the first time, the United manager had left Cristiano Ronaldo on the bench for a whole game in which they lost 6–3 to arch-rivals Manchester City.

"Ronaldo is on the bench *again*," David said, repeating what he had heard from fans in front of the stadium. "It makes no sense. They say we play better without him, but I don't see it that way. Ronaldo is still our best player, even now in his later footballing years. Why does the manager leave him out for the big games?"

"Cristiano must be dying inside at this point," said Edo. "He's not dealing well with the situation."

"Of course!" said David. "And rightfully so! He wants to prove he is still the best."

"Yep," said Edo. "And the situation Ten Hag has put him in recently doesn't go hand in hand with his idea of himself—the one who was *born to be the best*."

"El sueño del niño," said David, solemnly.

"Slow down, man," yelled Edo as David took off up the stairs towards the stand. "You know I can't go that fast with my hip!"

"Does it still hurt you?" David said, surprised.

"A little bit, man," said Edo. "That damn bicycle kick."

"Look at all these cameras," said David as they entered the corridor of the Sir Bobby Charlton stand. "There are more cameras than ever. And more rules also—don't do *this*, don't do *that*. It feels like they track our every move, especially since the pandemic. It feels like Big Brother is watching us. It's scary shit, my friend!"

"It's becoming more and more like football, isn't it?" said Edo with a half grin.

"What do you mean, man?" said David.

"Well, you know," said Edo. "In football, there's always a referee, following your every step and chasing you down. Imagine somebody chasing you around in your life, checking every step you take and bringing you to justice. That's what football is!"

"Well, that's exactly how society works, too," said David. "The state follows every step we take. Technology has increased the amount of control we are under. It took the romantic times away."

"Yep, just like football," said Edo. "You can't get away with *anything* anymore."

"Absolutely," said David. "*Damn*, VAR. You said it, Edo."

"I did, yeah," said Edo.

"We are always being *filmed and tracked*," said David. "Or, if you remember the situation from a couple of years ago, it's better to say *tracked and traced.* Isn't that right, government? They *really* made sure we didn't breach lockdown rules."

Edo nodded.

"And then there is the good, old audience," David continued. "Schools, friends and family who follow your every step, booing you and telling you off."

"Yeah, just like these ugly Manchester United fans," said Edo and laughed as they entered the stand, moving through the nervous crowd toward their seats.

"Even when it came to *neighbours*," David said, getting annoyed. "It was all about snitching you out to the state officials for going to the shop during self-isolation. They would do everything they could to catch you out."

Edo thought for a moment.

"To catch you out of life," he said suddenly. "Footballers also get sent off from life when they breach the rules, don't they, David? And when they commit a nasty tackle on another player, the audience will always shout loud enough to make sure the referee sends the player off."

"Fucking neighbours!" David yelled as they found their two empty seats in the middle of the ground with a good view of the United bench. "They can't mind their own business, but they'll pay for a ticket to have a nosy at yours!"

"Yep," said Edo as they sat down. David looked down at the players warming up.

"So if football is life, and a player gets sent off—from life," David said. "Does that mean a red card is *death*?"

Edo paused for a moment, looking around.

"Well, to find an answer to this question, David, we first need to agree on what death *is*. And here we go back to *identification*. Since football players don't generally die while playing football, we need to ask ourselves, what else can they lose if not their lives?"

"Yes!" said David, nodding. "What is worthy of their survival? Why are they winning? Why are they scoring goals?"

"Exactly!" said Edo. "That is the question, David. What part of them dies?"

David sat back and scanned the pitch, sensing Edo was about to expound on one of his theories.

"In my book," Edo began. "*Every* loss of identity is a death in itself. Whenever you experience the loss of something that *defines* you, a piece of you dies. A physical death is simply the ultimate de-identification with form."

David stared sadly at Cristiano Ronaldo warming up alone, away from the players and coaches.

"So yeah," said Edo. "A red card *is* death. If you ban a player from the field, you basically take away his sense of self, his sense of being a player—at least for a short time."

"And what does that make a ref?" said David. "God? Satan?"

Edo smiled.

"It depends on how you receive it," he said. "If the player accepts the red card, then it is the work of God." He looked David in the eyes. "Every death is an opportunity to look into yourself and to *allow* the change to happen. The change happens when you let go of the idea of *yourself*."

"And if you resist the red card?" said David.

"Well then, if you resist, that's where your over-identification with the role begins," said Edo. "You get stuck in misery and resentment, believing it's everybody else's fault, and everybody is your enemy, including the referee. And it's all an attempt to preserve the role you have created for yourself. If you resist, then the referee is *Satan*."

"But he also might just be a cocky policeman checking if you are self-isolating," said David.

They both laughed.

"The referee was definitely Satan from Cristiano's perspective when he got sent off in his first Juventus Champions League game against Valencia," Edo said, watching Ronaldo juggling the ball with his feet. "Oh my God, that was a proper act of dying! After three consecutive Champions League trophies with Real Madrid, he came to Juventus with the promise of another trophy. But instead, he was sent off in the twenty-ninth minute for pulling Valencia defender Jeison Murillo's hair."

"Devastating!" said David, shaking his head.

"He sure was devastated," said Edo. "Do you remember how he lay down on the pitch, sobbing and going completely mad? He wanted to keep playing. He didn't want to go to the other side of the line."

"He knew hell was waiting for him!" said David.

"Quite right," said Edo.

"My friend," said David, after a pause. "I can't think of a single player who humbly accepted the red card and remained at ease after being sent off."

Edo thought for a moment.

"Yeah, it doesn't happen often," he said. "That's because when players receive the red card, they are usually so controlled by ego and fear that they can't see the other side and thus accept that they've been sent off. They only see their own limited perspective of the situation. So, basically, they're in hell before the ref even sends them off. When Zidane headbutted Materazzi in the World Cup final 2006, he was already lost in his madness."

"Poor Materazzi was asking for it, though," said David.

"True," said Edo. "Materazzi was *always* looking to injure someone. There was some malice in his tackles. But you don't want to hurt others unless you are hurt yourself."

"And a few times, he got that fear mirrored back at him," said David. "Such as Zidane, Ibrahimović—"

"What happened with Ibrahimović?" asked Edo.

David leaned in as the volume of the crowd got louder.

"So," he said. "Materazzi tackled Ibrahimović badly in the 2006 Derby d'Italia, Juventus against Inter. Ibrahimović had to leave the pitch because he was so hurt. Then, later in the year, Zlatan left Juventus and joined Inter, where he played *with* Materazzi for three seasons. He never forgot about that tackle, though. And, eventually, Zlatan left Inter for Barcelona, where he stayed for a year before returning to Italy, this time at *AC* Milan."

"Oh, I see where this is going," said Edo.

"It was the first Milan derby of the season," said David. "Inter against Milan, and in the second half, Zlatan put Materazzi in hospital with a Taekwondo kick. Dejan Stanković asked Zlatan why he did it, and he said, *I've been waiting for this moment for four years. That's why.*"[29]

"Wow. That's *cold*," said Edo.

David nodded furiously.

"He only got a yellow, though," he said. "Just as Materazzi only got booked four years earlier. Both tackles would be straight reds in today's game."

"Yeah, times have changed," said Edo. "However, those were all moments of madness, just like Totti was lost in madness when he booted Balotelli in the Coppa Italia final and got sent off. Just as Ramos was lost in madness when he kicked Messi and then hit Puyol and Xavi in 2010, El Clásico. And on numerous other occasions."

"Like, when Cantona flying-kicked a Crystal Palace fan, he was already lost in his moment of madness," said David.

"Moments of hell, David," said Edo. "From the point of *madness*, the red card can only mean *salvation*. Death is salvation because it can only dissolve those layers of ego, de-identifying with a mad mind and bringing forth clarity once the player wakes up from the madness. And when you are alone in that locker room after you have been sent off, that is probably the loneliest place in the world. It's the right place to contemplate."

"So the ref is God, after all!" said David.

Fearless Zlatan Ibrahimović

Cojones of the Balkans, Skin of Scandinavia

"This is our best game of the season," said David as the second half began with United and Tottenham level at 0–0. "We need to keep doing what we are doing, and the goal will come."

"Ibrahimović!" said Edo, both randomly and nostalgically. "Do you remember when Ibrahimović played at Manchester United, David?"

"Of course I do, Edo," said David proudly. "Mourinho brought him here at the ripe old age of thirty-five. Ibra was *always* ready to die for Mou. And he played really well before that nasty knee injury stopped him towards the end of the season."

"And did you know," said Edo, "That was only the third time in sixteen seasons that he didn't win the league title for the club he played for?"

David stood up and placed an arm in the air dramatically.

"*I came, I saw, I conquered*," he said, quoting Zlatan Ibrahimović. "Before Man United, the only two he *didn't* win the league with in those sixteen seasons were Ajax in 2003 and Milan in 2012. Wow, what a career he's had!"

"He's seen some places, hasn't he?" said Edo. "Malmö, Ajax, Juventus, Inter, Barcelona, Milan, Paris, Manchester, LA Galaxy and then Milan again."

"Ibrahimović is one of a kind," said David. "In every possible way. That friendly against England when he scored four goals was something else. All four were absolute stunners, but that last one—that overhead kick from thirty meters was something the footballing world had never seen before—almost as good as yours, Edo. It was out of this world. Only Ibrahimović could make such a masterclass out of a friendly match."

Edo smiled and gave his hip a little massage.

"Thanks, David," he said. "And yeah, Zlatan has always been unique wherever he played. My favourite Ibrahimović phase was his first year at AC Milan. After the debacle in Barcelona, it seemed Milan was where he took his game to the next level. Milan was great. Paris was great. Juventus was great as well. He was great everywhere, actually—apart from Ajax and Barcelona, which were too structured for someone so wild."

"My favourite phase was Paris Saint-Germain!" said David. "He scored some ridiculous goals there."

Edo nodded his agreement and took out his usual flask of tea.

"Imagine what happens when you learn from so many different clubs, environments, people, coaches, managers," he said. "Imagine how rich the man is who carries the history of Ajax, the wisdom of the Old Lady, the ruthlessness of Inter, the creativity of Blaugrana, the calmness of Milan, the glory of Paris. And that's why he learnt to stand up for himself. Ibra is a survivor. He is an army unto himself. He carries the cojones of the Balkans, where he was born, *and* the thick skin of Scandinavia, where he grew up—bravery *and* resilience!"

"Get in there!" David leapt to his feet suddenly with the rest of the crowd, as Fred's shot got deflected and ended up in the back of the Spurs net. All around them was filled with a deafening roar and the madness of euphoria.

Edo stood clapping conservatively while David jumped around like a madman.

"This is our best game this season, without a shadow of a doubt," yelled David when he finally calmed down and began clapping normally like Edo. "Without a *shadow* of a doubt," he repeated.

"Look at Cristiano," shouted Edo, pointing at the United bench where Cristiano Ronaldo slumped with his arms crossed. "He doesn't look happy at all."

"Maybe we really *do* play better without him," said David, sounding a little shocked. "Ronaldo's biggest fears are turning into reality."

"All fears have their root in one single fear," said Edo.

"A fear of death?" said David.

"That's right, David," said Edo as they sat down. "In the fear of *death*. Cristiano ultimately fears losing his *self-created* idea of himself—because *who is he*, if not the most important player in the team? If not the best scorer in the league? If not the implacable CR7? The answer to these questions, David, is what Cristiano fears most—what his ego fears most."

"Well," muttered David. "He is less—"

"Less what?"

"Less of a human, I guess."

"Yes, but he is also *more* of a human being," said Edo. "But *only* if he can let *the image* go. People use fear as a shield to protect the character they have created. They don't want anything to challenge that character. The current situation, with him on the bench, is massively challenging Cristiano's CR7 identity. And he can't allow that image to die—not after he has put so much into it. Just as he can't betray the people around him who have put a lot of effort into enhancing that image. He doesn't want to lose his identity, which makes them see him as a god. If one cannot let it go, it means fear is taking over and manifesting as anxiety, anger, aggression, or something else."

"Aggression? Like Ivan Gennaro Gattuso?" David said.

"There you go," said Edo.

"So what are you trying to say?" said David, screwing up his face. "Gattuso is afraid?"

"Absolutely, man," said Edo. "Gattuso *is* afraid! Every time he starts a fight, he is fighting his own fear to preserve that angry character he created."

"But he wouldn't be Gattuso if he wasn't fighting," said David. "All that he is, he owes to his character—to his craziness. Opponents were terrified of him. When he stepped on the pitch and shouted from the bottom of his lungs, players from other teams would shudder."

"Exactly," said Edo. "Because fear is infectious, David. It spreads like a *virus*. That's why dealing with fear should be everybody's civic duty. Because if you don't deal with your fear, it simply reflects in others. Milan players told a story about one occasion where Ibrahimović picked up Gattuso and threw him in the bin after Gattuso mocked him for a whole training session."[30]

"Ibra really dealt with the Italian gangster," laughed David.

"Indeed," said Edo. "Cojones of the Balkans, my friend, cojones of the Balkans."

"But what about *football*?" said David. "I mean, like I said, Gattuso wouldn't be a football player if he didn't have that fear factor—if he didn't create that *aggressive* character."

"True," said Edo. "But in reality, he's much bigger than the role he identifies with."

"What? So, he's also Ronaldinho?" said David.

"Correct, David," said Edo. "He *is* Ronaldinho. Essentially, we are *all* Ronaldinho. But only if we can recognise and differentiate our ego from our true selves. Otherwise, when the moment of change arrives, fear will only enhance our identity and instead of letting it go, we will identify even more with what we have lost. We will feel regret and sorrow and spread misery."

Edo and David both stared at Ronaldo for a moment.

"You see, it's pure torture for Cristiano," said Edo. "And subsequently for the rest of the players who share the locker room with him."

"Well, fear can be good if we use it appropriately," said David. "Actually, because of that fear, players can perform at the highest level. I bake the best bread in my street because I'm afraid of what I am if I'm not the best baker. I'm the loudest fan of Man United because I'm afraid of losing that feeling of *belonging*. Gattuso is the scariest motherfucker because he's afraid of not being scary. Ronaldo is the best because he's afraid of not being the best. He needs to fight for himself somehow. He—" David paused. His face softened in a moment of compassion for the great man. "Ronaldo's entire *legacy* is at stake—his entire *life*!"

Edo nodded softly.

"You're right, David. His entire life is at stake. As Alex Ferguson accurately said in his book, *When you don't play them, you are taking their life away.*"[31]

"Sir Alex *always* played him," said David.

"Interestingly, Zlatan and Cristiano had similar career paths, in one sense," said Edo. "They both returned to their old clubs in their late footballing years. But unlike Cristiano, Zlatan accepted his position in the team, which is often on the bench. And from his place on the bench, he can still influence the game so much. At the end of last season, at the grand old age of thirty-eight, he was the main factor in Milan winning that last Scudetto, ending eleven painful years of waiting for the title. After winning that title, his speech in the dressing room showed us everything we need to know about Ibrahimović. He flipped the table over while screaming: *Milano non é Milan. Italia é Milan*—Italy is AC Milan."[32]

"He *promised* he would get Milan the title one last time, and he did it," said David.

"And he did it without the key ligament in his knee!" Edo added. "He was rewarded for *accepting* his situation."

"It's funny because he has never won the Champions League," said David. "He hasn't even been close. I don't think he's ever even played in a semi-final."

"Maybe this year!" said Edo.

"Sure," said David. "If he gets back from the injury!"

"Indeed," said Edo. "After the last season, while recovering from an operation, he said he doesn't fear not returning to football. He said, *If I don't manage to return, I don't manage. You have to be ready for all outcomes.*"[33]

"Fear?" said David.

"Fear, David."

"So basically, he's not afraid to lose the character of Zlatan Ibrahimović—the football player?"

"Yes, that's my point, man," said Edo. "Which makes me think that he's not that egoistic after all."

"Really?" said David. "I mean, he literally calls himself a *god*. He calls himself *football*. What are we talking about here, Edo? It sounds like a pretty strong ego to me! Ibra once said if he weren't egoistic, he would be a simple player and that he didn't *see himself* as a simple player. *When I am on the field, I have to do my things. I have to score my goals. I have to create the chances. To do that, you need to be a little egoistic because ego is also a quality*."[34]

"Right," said Edo. "His liberation from fear probably only came as he matured. But I always found him more of a guy consciously playing the role of a god rather than somebody who believed he was God himself. He's always been a bit of a joker."

"Yeah, maybe," said David. "You never really know with Ibrahimović."

"He's a bit of a mystic, too," said Edo. "He picked up some of that mysticism from everywhere he went. Life is too short to stay in one place. Life happens *outside* the comfort zone—when you step into the *uncertainty*—when you keep challenging everything you know about yourself—when you keep dying and being reborn again and again."

How to Get Into Someone's Head

A Goalie's Lecture

Edo finally poured two teas from the flask he'd held for a long time. David took a cup and immediately spilt some down his trousers.

"Why am I not surprised?" Edo laughed.

David smiled, wiping off the tea, taking a sip and sitting back.

"So, Edo," he said. "We've established that football players need to have big egos. And therefore, they need fear as well to keep them going. Because of fear, Ronaldo is what he is."

Edo screwed the lid on the flask and put it back in his bag.

"It's funny because what we often perceive as mental strength is nothing but fear-motivated action," Edo said. "You don't want to lose the character you have built, so you keep pushing to preserve it. But since fear is the root of so-called mental strength, that mental strength must have a *serious* flip side."

"Yeah," said David. "But because of that fear, Ronaldo is ruthless when it comes to penalties. He can't afford to miss and, therefore, to become less. We agreed once that penalties are a mirror of the mental state."

"True," said Edo. "His actions that are controlled by fear are perceived as mental strength. However, there's a different type of mental strength—one that comes from stillness rather than fear. And therefore, it doesn't have a flip side. It's the mental strength known by those who can see beyond winning and losing."

"Goaaal!" David leapt to his feet, dropping his tea on the floor as Bruno Fernandes buried the ball in the Spurs net from the edge of the box.

The whole crowd erupted again. And after a minute or so of euphoric madness, David joined Edo in his conservative clapping once more.

"That's what I'm talking about!" said David. "This is how we should always play. It's our best game of the season by miles!"

"Lloris is so pissed off," said Edo. "He wants more protection from his outfield players."

A group of United players ran after Fernandes on the opposite side of the pitch to Edo and David.

"Lloris always looks so angry with that huge wrinkle between his eyes," Edo said. "One would think he might have a decent penalty save record, but it's the opposite. His poor penalty rate proves that penalty takers don't care about his angry face."

"Yeah, because he doesn't know how to exploit that angry face," said David.

"Some proven goalkeepers are more efficient at saving penalties than others," said Edo.

"Yes, they are," said David. "And so what?"

Edo thought about it.

"You said last year that goalkeepers don't play any role in the success or failure of penalties," he said. "You said that it's all down to the mental strength of the penalty *taker*. But there are clearly goalies who players are afraid of. The first one who comes to mind is Tim Krul, the Dutch keeper. He *always* manages to get into a player's head. Krul had a remarkable performance at the 2014 World Cup in Brazil. In the quarter-final against Costa Rica, they subbed him on thirty seconds before the end of extra time. And he saved two penalties in the shootout, helping the Netherlands into the semi-final."

"Yeah, but—"

"Or," continued Edo. "A more recent example occurred in the fifth round of the 2020 FA Cup between Spurs and Norwich. It was just before the pandemic paralysed the world."

"Pre-COVID Tottenham?" said David. "Correct me if I'm wrong, Edo, but that sounds like Mourinho's Tottenham."

"Yes, I think you are correct," said Edo. "And after extra time, the result was 1–1, and they went to penalties. And straight away, Norwich's Tim Krul stole the show. He had a water bottle with the names of the Spurs players and their most likely penalty placements written on it. Krul's antics included talking to penalty takers, bouncing on the line, shaking the crossbar, clapping, and hitting the post. He tried to do whatever it took to obstruct the penalty takers. And *that's* the role of a goalkeeper when it comes to penalties, David. His role is to get into the taker's head—to rock the stability they bring to the white spot—to make them face their fears. It's a mental game."

"Goalies are made different," said David, standing up as United nearly scored again.

"They absolutely are," said Edo. "Their role is so different to any other role in football. You know what they say, David—*If goalkeepers were sane, they wouldn't be restricted to a sixteen-metre box.* And I believe their own insanity helps them reach the insane part of the penalty taker's mind."

David nodded.

"So how did it go?" he asked. "With Krul?"

"How did it go, pal?" said Edo. "Three saved penalties out of five. Not bad, right? Actually, one of those wasn't even saved—the ball went way over the crossbar."

"Yeah, the guy who hits the crossbar is scared," said David.

"That one can be considered the ultimate win of the goalkeeper," said Edo, laughing. "Because when a goalie gets into the taker's head, suddenly the goalie seems really big, and the goal gets smaller."

"That's right," said David.

The two stood up as a man shuffled past with his young son.

"So you see," said Edo. "The keeper has a *significant* role when it comes to penalties."Remember a while ago when we talked about *The Green Mile* and the guy whose brain they cooked on the electric chair?"

"The mouse guy?" said David.

"Yeah. He got into that sadistic guy Percy's head," said Edo. "I mean, it couldn't have been difficult to get into that weak head anyway. But since he got into it, the sadistic executioner did the job terribly wrong and burnt the guy alive."

"Yeah," said David. "I didn't say keepers don't have a role. I said they don't have a purpose when a mentally superior player is in front of them. That's when a goalkeeper is the guy in the electric chair waiting to be executed. The lever drops, and two thousand volts melts the keeper's brain, neatly and effectively."

David pulled an air lever down and pretended to be zapped.

"Simple as that," he said, laughing. "And Rickie Lambert was the most efficient penalty taker of them all. He once said he sees a penalty as a free shot from twelve yards, and a professional should score from that distance *ten times out of ten*, so if you hit it well, you'll be alright. *I try and hit the penalty as if I know the goalkeeper is going that way as well. So if he does, he still won't be able to save it,* he said."[35]

"That's good advice," said Edo, thinking about it.

"So you see, mate, not even the mastermind Krul could sabotage a *firm* penalty taker," David said. "Tell me, who were the players that missed penalties in that shootout against Krul?"

Edo pulled out his phone and began searching on Google. And now the pair were forced to shout their conversation as the United fan songs became deafening.

"Erik Lamela," Edo shouted. "Also, Troy Parrott and one more guy—Gedson Fernandes!"

"Well, that's my point," David yelled back. "Who the fuck are those guys? They're the kind of players who aren't mentally developed, that's who. And as such, they are prone to freeze up, giving seasoned professionals like Tim Krul permission to invade their heads and cause them to fail."

"Maybe, yeah," Edo said as the crowd calmed down.

"Let me give you a good example," said David. "It was the Derby della Madonnina in 2012, and the beautiful stadium, San Siro, was packed with crazy Italian fans. The Inter keeper, Júlio César, tackled Kevin-Prince Boateng in the box, giving a penalty to AC Milan. Zlatan Ibrahimović stepped up and put the ball on the spot. Everything was ready for the execution. But Julio César started controlling the show. And he knew it had to be the show of his life if he wanted to get into Ibrahimović's impenetrable head—"

David got excited and stood up, animating his story above Edo's head.

"The ball was on the spot," he said. "But César turned his back to Ibrahimović. Then, after a few seconds, he left the pitch, pretending to be in pain. Ibrahimović was ready to shoot, but the keeper wasn't on his line. César took more time to fix up his equipment before he finally decided to return. And Ibrahimović was ready, but César walked out towards him."

"What? Wow!" said Edo.

"Ibra didn't want to look at him, but he had no choice when César came close and whispered something. Zlatan wasn't paying any attention. César moved away from him saying, *I know you are going to hit it hard in the centre of the goal.* Something like that.[36] But still, Ibra didn't pay any attention."

Edo stood up next to David now.

"The real question is," Edo said, "Did Zlatan not pay attention because he was *beyond* that drama or because he was like Cristiano, desperate to avoid failure? Was he afraid or not afraid? Does his mental strength come from fear or *stillness*? And in what percentage? I believe a lot of Ibra's mental strength comes from stillness."

"And do you know what happened next?" said David.

"Go on."

"César stuck his tongue out at Ibrahimović," said David, getting overexcited. "But Ibra *still* wasn't paying attention. César finally returned to his line, did a few more tricks, and that was it."

"That was what?" said Edo.

"The judge made his verdict," said David. "The offender was in the electric chair. The executioner was ready to pull the lever."

David glared into Edo's eyes.

"And?" said Edo.

"*BAAAM,*" said David, pulling down on his imaginary lever. "Two thousand volts straight to the offender's head."

The Case of Mario Balotelli

Twenty-Six Converted Penalties in a Row

David looked satisfied, with his lips stretched out in a smile, and he was subtly nodding as he watched the game.

"I've got only one problem regarding my penalty theory," David said suddenly. He swung around and looked directly at Edo. "Mario Balotelli!"

"Oh yeah?" said Edo, his eyes on the game. "What about him?"

"Well, mate, he challenges my theory that penalties are a mirror of the mental state. I mean, he is a top penalty taker, isn't he?—one of the best, you might say. Don't you think, Edo?"

"I would agree with that," Edo confirmed. "But so what?"

"So what?" said David, his look of satisfaction giving way to one of irritation. "Obviously, he's not a mentally *stable* person. His mental strength doesn't come from fear *no*r stillness. It's non-existent, my friend. He's like that mouse killer in the Green Mile!"

"Why would you say that?" said Edo, who calmly continued watching the game.

"Come on, dude," said David, throwing his arms up. "Mourinho once said he could write a two-hundred-page book about his two years at Inter with Mario. He also said the book wouldn't be a drama but a *comedy*."

"Oh, Mou!" said Edo, waving his hand dismissively. "Why does it always come back to Mou?"

"Seriously," said David. "On one occasion, Inter played Rubin Kazan in the Champions League, and all of Mourinho's strikers were injured—no Diego Milito, no Samuel Eto'o. Balotelli was the only one left. And he got booked just before half-time. When Mourinho entered the dressing room at the break, he spent fourteen minutes of the fifteen-minute break speaking only to Mario. He told him, *Mario, I cannot change you. I have no strikers on the bench, so don't touch anybody and play only with the ball. If we lose the ball, no reaction. If someone provokes you, no reaction. If the referee makes a mistake, no reaction. Mario—please.*"[37]

"Boring," said Edo.

"A *forty-sixth* minute red card!" shouted David.

"Ahh, Mourinho!" said Edo, waving his friend away again. "First of all, David, you are exaggerating. It wasn't the forty-sixth minute, but later in the half. Secondly, Mourinho didn't know how to deal with Balotelli. If he knew better, he wouldn't have spent fourteen minutes speaking to him because he would have known this speech would have had the opposite effect."

"No, man," insisted David. "It's *not* about Mourinho. It's about Balotelli. We're talking about a guy who threw darts at the Manchester City youth players for fun."

"Oh, come on! Shit happens," said Edo.

"What? Shit happens?" said David. "This guy burnt down his bathroom after shooting fireworks from his window. Who got caught trespassing at a women's prison? Who got in *countless* fights with his teammates, opponents, referees, coaches, and fans? Who, Edo? Anyone can see that Mario isn't mentally stable."

"Well," said Edo, grinning. "He was on converted penalty number *twenty-six* before he finally missed the first in his career. "So you can't deny he must have some mental stability."

"You bastard, Edo," said David. "You're using my theory against me! And I don't like it!"

"Be careful what you say, then," said Edo.

"Mate," said David, pausing for dramatic effect. "This man threw darts at his junior colleagues! Don't you listen?"

"Even Tim Krul couldn't save his penalty," Edo said, casually watching the game. "Manchester City versus Newcastle, 2011. Balotelli versus Krul. Oh, that was a clash of the penalty titans! Tim Krul knew who he was facing, for sure. He tried all his usual tricks. But he was helpless when Mario stepped up at his slow pace and did his famous tiny stop to confuse the keeper. He followed it up with a soft shot to the keeper's left. Krul didn't even *move*."

David muttered to himself.

"Sounds stable to me!" said Edo.

"I'm just not sure anymore," said David.

"Balotelli even tried to get in Krul's face as revenge, but the Dutchman turned his back," Edo said.

"That sounds unstable if you ask me," said David. "He had everything he could wish for, and he still pulled shit like that."

"Yes," said Edo. "And all of his success is down to him. God knows it wasn't an easy road for Mario. Clearly, some of his actions are driven by his trauma, but let him have some fun. If his way out is having fun through rebellion, the least we can do is to accept him as he comes."

"He could have been among the best in the world if he wasn't so interested in seeking fun," said David, now facing the game again.

"Well, look," said Edo. "It's not like he owes it to you or anyone to become the best footballer in the world. And he's overcome way harder challenges than that anyway."

"There's no tougher challenge than becoming the best footballer in the world," said David. "Not even the likes of Paul Scholes made it, by the way."

"Forget about Scholes now," barked Edo. "Balotelli did something way tougher. He fought *rejection* over and over again."

"Ahhh, here we go again," said David, becoming irritated.

"You know, David," said Edo. "Mario was born in Sicily to Ghanaian immigrants. He was born with intestinal problems, and his parents couldn't properly care for their sick child, so they gave him up for foster care. Soon, the Balotelli family adopted Mario and brought him to the North of Italy, to Brescia."

"Well, I know a few people who grew up in a foster family," said David.

"Yep," said Edo, "But can you imagine what it means to be left by your parents in a foreign country? They moved him to a town where he was among a few black children—in an overwhelmingly white environment. Can you imagine being rejected by your parents and then by your environment?"

"As far as I'm aware," said David. "The Balotelli family gave him all the love he needed. I mean, he even has their names engraved on his boots."

"Well, we can't really know about that," said Edo. "Regardless, the influence of the environment was stronger than any love he received. Mario was keenly aware that he didn't look the same as his white siblings. It led to challenging questions about the nature of his identity. Obviously, he didn't have the wisdom to seek his true self within."

"Oh, come on," said David. "You might be overreacting."

"People have written stories claiming that Balotelli grew obsessed with the colour of his skin," said Edo. "They say he either shaded it in pink with pens or scrubbed his hands with boiling water to get them clean."[38]

"Hmm, that's harsh," said David, lowering his head.

"Do you see my point now?" said Edo. "Rejection!"

David shook his head and soberly leaned forward.

"Yeah, I hear you, Edo," he said. "But I still can't figure out how that makes him mentally stable."

"Think about rejection," said Edo. "Who does that word remind you of?"

David paused momentarily before glancing again at Ronaldo on the United bench.

"CR7," David whispered.

"That's right, David," said Edo. "And in some cases, trauma makes you keep going, fighting and finding a particular focus point from where you can operate on what is perceived as a high mental level. However, if that strength doesn't come from within—from a place of stillness—that same strength will manifest as fear in other situations that life throws at you. That's why having mental strength doesn't necessarily mean a person is liberated from mental weakness when it comes to penalties. We can see it with both Cristiano and Balotelli."

"I still don't agree Balotelli is mentally stable in any case," said David.

Edo thought for a moment.

"Do you know the major difference between Cristiano and Mario?" he said.

"Yeah, I know!" said David. "Ronaldo is the best in the world, and Balotelli is far from that!"

"True!" said Edo. "But do you know why that is? I mean, they both sought consolation in football. But do you know what Balotelli found instead?"

"What's that?" said David.

"He found more rejection," said Edo. "Only this time, it was the fans who rejected him."

David nodded soberly again, and Edo turned to face his friend.

"Mario received racial abuse during his first professional game for Lumezzane," said Edo. "He was fifteen years old, and as we know, monkey noises made by supporters have never truly gone away. Mario might not even know it, but he has grown and progressed with rejection."

"Ok, Edo," David said. "I understand all that. I understand that Balotelli had a difficult life. I understand he has been rejected since birth. But in my opinion, all that stuff made him nuts and mentally unstable, rather than mentally stable."

"Ahh, you just don't see it," said Edo.

"No, I don't," said David. "I mean, after everything he has gone through, and after all the crazy shit he has done as a player and as a human, how can you still claim all that stuff made him mentally stable while everything points to him being crazy?"

"Well, David," said Edo, turning back to watch the game. "Mourinho said that the book about Mario would be a comedy rather than a tragedy. And if Mou can change his perspective for once, then maybe all of us can, too."

Trauma—The Profoundest Lesson

When Priorities Reshuffle

The game was coming to an end. United were 2–0 up against Tottenham, and several United players were warming up next to the pitch.

"This isn't fair," said David as he looked longingly at Cristiano Ronaldo, who was still on the bench. "A couple of weeks ago, when we lost 6–3 to City, Ten Hag said that he had not subbed Ronaldo in out of respect."[39]

"Yeah. He wanted to spare him the misery," said Edo.

"So why does he not play him now when we are winning?" said David. "Sometimes football can be traumatic."

Edo nodded solemnly.

"Trauma comes in both physical and mental forms," he said. "Interestingly, Cristiano has always avoided serious *physical* traumas."

"That's true," said David. "And God knows football can be rough! There have been some truly horrible injuries throughout the game's history—some serious physical traumas. But I suppose injuries are part of the game, aren't they? I mean, trauma is a part of life. It's what makes life so unpredictable. And let's be honest. Football is a physical game. That's what makes it so great. We couldn't have such an intense game without injuries."

"True," said Edo. "It's also what makes football so relatable to life. Would we even be sitting here right now if the game didn't have injuries? Life is a risk, David. And the more you risk, the more interesting life becomes."

"That's why the Premier League is the most famous league in the world," said David. "It's because the game flows. Referees don't call fouls for every contact. They let the game go on as much as possible. It's also what makes the Premier League so intense. But on the other hand, it makes it more prone to injuries—to *trauma*, as well. And we *love* it."

Edo nodded his agreement.

"From the limited egoic perspective, some profound life events can be perceived as bad and as huge setbacks on our paths," he said. "But they can also be a platform for a significant shift of consciousness if we don't identify with them, seeing them instead for what they really are. Identifying with the trauma will only cause us pain and suffering when, in reality, the trauma offers us an opportunity to experience insight into ourselves."

"Yeah," said David. "And it's not like we choose to have trauma. It's *always* there."

"Absolutely, David," said Edo. "It's always there *unless* you stay in your comfort zone and don't expose yourself to new challenges, like if you keep playing against the same familiar opponents week in and week out. But that's not how you grow and learn. Trauma can be seen as a profound lesson."

"Yes, my friend," said David. "Injuries are tough, nonetheless! My thoughts are with those who haven't yet found a way to add some positivity to their traumatic situations."

"No question about that!" agreed Edo.

"We have all witnessed an injury or tackle that will stay with us forever," said David. "What's yours, Edo? Aside from your hip injury from your overhead kick, of course!"

"Of course," said Edo, grinning. He paused for a moment in thought, then said, "Mine is Eduardo da Silva."

"Uhh," said David, shaking his head. "That was a tough one. And what a player he was before the injury! I'll never forget his goal against England during that 2008 Euro qualifier in Zagreb. Niko Kovač crossed a balloon in the air, and Eduardo positioned himself between John Terry and Ashley Cole to lob the keeper with his head. Croatia won 2–0 in Zagreb, then 3–2 at Wembley a year later, to leave England short of the Euros. And then Martin Taylor's tackle happened—Birmingham versus Arsenal, 2008."

David took a deep breath and shook his head.

"Correct," said Edo. "Da Silva didn't experience Euro 2008 in Austria and Switzerland, even though he got ten goals in the qualifiers. The man paved the way for Croatia to get there, but that injury was the end for him."

"Actually, it wasn't the end," said David. "He returned after a year and scored two goals on his return debut against Cardiff City."

"True," said Edo. "But he never played at the same level as before his injury—not even close. He even had a decent career at Shakhtar Donetsk later, but he was just a shadow of his former self. He just never fully recovered. Plus, he had so many setback injuries that kept him from scoring how he had scored before."

David scratched his head. "I guess the trauma made him weaker rather than stronger after all," he said.

"Well, that's not true," said Edo. "It might have made him less of a football player, but he came out of it a much stronger human being. If I recall correctly, years after Eduardo's injury, he took a stand against the president of Dinamo Zagreb, Eduardo's first European club. What was that about again?"

"Zdravko Mamić was the president's name," David said. "And yes, Eduardo was the only football player brave enough to stand up against Zdravko, the big boss of Croatian football and Dinamo. Mamić claimed Eduardo owed him money over his contract, which entitled Mamić to a big chunk of Eduardo's earnings once he left Dinamo Zagreb. Mamić sued Eduardo for not paying him his part. And even though no one had ever pushed back against Mamić, because he is the big boss of Croatian football—a *very* scary guy, Eduardo counter-sued Mamić, claiming the contract was usurious because Eduardo didn't speak Croatian when he first came from Brazil to sign the contract at eighteen years old. In the end, Eduardo lost and had to pay Mamić one million euros or something like that.[40] Mamić's influence was too big at that point—even on judges."

"Yeah, clearly, football was not Eduardo's focus anymore," said Edo. "However, I firmly believe if it *had* been, he would have come back as a better footballing person as well. Sometimes, horrific injuries make players change their style or even change their position on the pitch. Ultimately, it can even make them change their role, as was the case with Ryan Mason, who retired as a player after Gary Cahill broke his skull. Mason found a new drive as a coach. Sometimes it takes years, though, for the new, reinvented world, born out of trauma, to start producing fruit."

"Yeah, maybe football really is about mere survival, sometimes," said David, smiling at his friend.

Edo smiled back.

"It really is, man," he said.

Edo pointed down at Ryan Mason, sitting on the Tottenham bench, next to Antonio Conte.

"When Mourinho left Tottenham," said Edo. "Mason became interim manager of Spurs, and as a twenty-nine-year-old became the youngest manager to ever lead a Premier League club. He might get back as a first-team coach again!"

"I can see him coming," said David, nodding.

"But yeah," said Edo. "Trauma sometimes changes your life priorities. It can make you realise what matters, and you no longer prioritise football."

"Yes, but Edo," said David. "What is more important than football? Than *life*?"

Edo grinned.

"For Eduardo, it was his family," Edo said. "During his first interview after the injury, he said that he could now focus on his family and that he was finding happiness in such *homely* moments.[41] His wife Andrea helped him overcome the injury. They've been together for more than twenty years, from the earliest days of his arrival in Croatia."

"*Love*, my friend, isn't it?" said David.

Edo nodded.

"Arsenal fans loved him as well," he continued. "Before the injury, they loved him. But when he returned after injury, he was the most loved player. The tragedy changed everybody involved, David—Eduardo da Silva, his family, his teammates, Arsène Wenger, Arsenal fans and so on. Tragedy brought people together. And let's not forget the man who broke his leg—Martin Taylor."

"The Butcher!" said David with a grimace.

"Well, he *must* have been devastated as well," said Edo. "His situation was no less difficult than Eduardo's. *No less!* And it can't have helped that people called him 'The Butcher'. And Arsène Wenger calling for Taylor's lifetime suspension didn't help either. Taylor received death threats daily and struggled to deal with the situation. He was devastated. Just *imagine* how he felt after that tackle, sitting alone in a locker room, knowing he might have ended his colleague's career. The locker room is scary when you are sitting there alone after getting sent off. But imagine how scary it is, sitting alone after breaking someone's leg. To accept that situation—that's a *big* one, David—to accept both your red card *and* the possible ending of a man's career."

"It was difficult for everybody," said David, hanging his head.

"Yes!" said Edo. "And everybody became wiser from it as well."

"Yep," said David. "Let's face it, Edo, life is a risk. And, as harsh as it sounds, football is also a risk, and that's what makes it beautiful!"

Edo patted his friend on the back.

"Absolutely, David," he said.

No Role Is Permanent

It's Time to Move On

Erik ten Hag made two substitutions in the eighty-seventh minute of the game, and Cristiano Ronaldo was *not* one of them. David couldn't help but show his disappointment despite United being 2–0 up. He sat down and hung his head for a moment in thought.

"So, my friend," David began. "We established at some point that football clubs need both wins and losses to improve—to *evolve*. We also established that lessons come after defeats. That being the case, why don't managers get more time before they get sacked?"

"Well, I suppose that's the million-dollar question," said Edo, shrugging his shoulders. "Football is an extraordinary world these days. Greed controls the game, pal. And it's challenging to be wise when money writes the terms of agreement. Too many people are involved who want it all and want it now, as in the Queen song. There's no wisdom."

"Life—" David muttered. "It's only a matter of time before that bubble of greed will burst, and the game as we know it will cease to exist."

Edo shrugged his shoulders again as if he had accepted the situation.

"Robert Prosinečki changed a few clubs as a manager," Edo said. "On a couple of occasions, Prosinečki said that there are only two types of managers—those who have been sacked and those who are yet to be sacked."[42]

"Hah, what a great man!" said David.

"I'll always remember the 1998 World Cup in France when Croatia won the bronze medal," said Edo. "Prosinečki played great the whole tournament and famously scored against the Netherlands in the match for third place. He spun around beautifully in the box to shake off two Dutch defenders and smashed it into the far corner of Van der Sar's goal. It was one of the most precious Croatian goals in history. That goal became part of the nation's folklore and was a cornerstone for the miracle that Modrić and the rest of the Croatian team would deliver twenty years later in Russia."

"So *two types of coaches*, yeah?" said David.

"Yep," said Edo. "The sacked ones and ones who are yet to be sacked, which is essentially true. There are two types of men: those who are dead and those who are yet to die." Edo laughed. "Or coaches whose coaching identity has already died and those yet to undergo that process."

David sat up, still staring down at the United bench.

"Those who have been sacked and those who are *yet* to be sacked," he muttered.

"There's something profound in those words," said Edo. "It points to the impermanence of all things. If a human cultivates an awareness that all roles and structures have their expiry date, they can reach a state of mind free of external needs. With such wisdom comes a clarity that you are not less of a human being if you lose a job. You are already *complete*. Only then can you maintain the joy of the game wherever life takes you next and in whatever position it puts you—as a pundit, coach or a manager."

"Or you can just take it as a lesson!" said David.

"Or you can just take it as a lesson," repeated Edo quietly. "Fear emerges when you can't de-identify with the role. Do you remember, David? What will I be if I cannot find a managerial position on the same level? Is that a failure?"

"Look! Look!" David said suddenly.

Edo looked at the pitch to see Cristiano Ronaldo walking towards the dressing room.

"What's going on?" Edo said as the whole stadium stared at Cristiano Ronaldo.

"Is he leaving the pitch before the end?" said David, shocked.

"It seems so, David," said Edo as Ronaldo disappeared down the tunnel.

"Unbelievable!" said David. "This will not end well, I'm afraid."

"You see," said Edo, still staring at the tunnel as if Ronaldo might re-emerge. "*That's* the fear I'm talking about. What am I if I'm not a coach? What am I if I'm not a player? What am I if I don't play? What am I if not the great CR7? That's when it gets unbearably difficult, David."

"Yeah, that's tough," said David.

"You once said that Totti admitted to being afraid when finishing his career," said Edo.

"Yeah," said David. "He was scared. He spoke to seventy thousand people at the stadium that day. He said, T*his is not the same fear you feel when standing in front of the goal, and you are about to take a penalty. Allow me to be afraid. This time, it's me who needs you and your support.*"

"You see," said Edo. "Totti couldn't let go of the huge role he carried—that of the Prince of Rome, national hero and the strongest of all—the role of a football player. When they get sacked or finish their careers, they have two options. The first one is to become free of external structures and roles and to discover their full potential while continuing to dance with life as a partner."

"Or?" said David as if he already knew the answer. "What's the second option?"

"Or," said Edo. "They can get stuck in the role they have lost—stuck in the past, and they can keep living out some role that's not sustainable anymore. Thus, they create problems for themselves and others. Just as Cristiano is making it difficult for himself, his teammates, his manager, and you at the moment, David."

"It's not easy to let it go," said David. "Arafat's bakery is nearly bankrupt these days, and I see him struggling to let it go. His face looks different. He only feels good when he's baking bread. We *need* Arafat as well. He drives me forward! His bakery makes my bakery better. We need competition."

"Mourinho has never been able to let go of his role of *The Special One* either," said Edo.

"Oh, here we go," said David, throwing his arms in the air. "Mourinho, again? Really, my friend?"

"And since he has never been able to let go," Edo continued. "He brings his personal issues and fear to every club he joins. He just can't let go of his fear of losing *The Special One*—the man who gave him *everything*. But in the end, the man who also *took* everything *from him*. He could never fulfil his true potential due to that burden of ego. If he could have let it go, he might have realised his role as a manager is just another identification with form and that he is much bigger than the role of *The Special*

One. And if he could de-identify with that form, he could free himself from fear. Then he could start a fresh chapter at a new club with a new perspective, deeper wisdom, and a new, advanced role."

"Didn't he do that at Roma?" said David.

"I'm not sure if he did," said Edo.

David scratched his head again.

"He won the Europa Conference League in his first season," he said. "Another trophy to his name!"

"Yes, I know that," said Edo. "He made that clear to everybody with a tattoo on his arm."

"What tattoo?"

"You don't know?" said Edo. "José got a tattoo depicting all the European trophies he has acquired—Europa Conference included. It's on his arm for everyone to see. I mean, seriously? Is the Conference League title something somebody who calls himself *The Special One* should brag about?"

David screwed up his nose.

"Well, if the tattoo shows all his trophies," he said. "Then don't forget to mention the Champions League and Europa League trophies as well, mate."

"Exactly," said Edo. "It's next to those big trophies, which proves Mourinho's huge decline in achievements. With that tattoo, he wanted to show that he was still *The Special One* because he was the first manager to win all three European trophies. But come on. Is that special, or does Mourinho want us to *believe* it's special? I mean, the Conference League, David. Is that even a real competition?"

"Well, it was a real competition for him!" said David. "Before the final match against Feyenoord, when he was asked the same thing, he simply said, *This is our Champions League*."[43]

"Ok, so finally, he changed his perspective," Edo said. "He made such a huge deal of playing in the final of the Conference League against Feyenoord that people actually bought what he was saying. I wouldn't be surprised if UEFA made him a special ambassador of the competition—*The Special Ambassador*."

"Ahh, you just can't give him any credit, can you, Edo?" said David.

"He still clings to the image of *The Special One* and can't let it go," said Edo. "That's all I'm saying."

"It's a big image!" said David.

"It is a big image," said Edo. "But at this point, it's dragging him down, limiting him heavily. He can't unlock his true potential while stuck in the past."

"Sure," said David. "But at least he *has* a big past!"

"There are two types of coaches," said Edo. "Ones who are dead and ones who are yet to die." He looked, once again, at the tunnel where Ronaldo had disappeared and not returned. "And there are two types of players, David. There are those who have aged and those who are yet to age. Move on, Cristiano. You're old. It's time to accept it."

BALANCE

Wembley, London

February 2023

◇

Between Ronaldo and Ronaldinho

In the Service of Football

It was the end of February, and the English winter was still holding on tight. The new year, 2023, had brought tectonic shifts in the football world.

Lionel Messi was finally a world champion with Argentina, while Cristiano Ronaldo played for Saudi Arabian club Al-Nassr after Manchester United terminated his contract following Ronaldo's public criticism of the club and manager Erik ten Hag.

After seventeen years in charge of the club, the Glazer family had put Manchester United up for sale. Since the World Cup break in December, United had played eighteen games under Ten Hag, losing only once, making them the most in-form club in England. United were in third place in the Premier League, only five points behind leaders, Arsenal.

Edo and David sat on a bus together, travelling from Manchester to London for a meeting of old rivals Manchester United and Newcastle United in the League Cup final.

Que sera, sera, sang the bus full of Manchester United fans as they approached Victoria station in London—*whatever will be, will be, we're going to Wembley. Que sera, sera.*

"Ahh, good old London!" said Edo, noticing a carriage pulled by two black horses crossing the road.

"I can't believe we've come this far after the way this season started," said David deliriously. "Spirits are so high since the Glazer bastards decided to sell the club. It's obvious this success is down to that!"

"Come on," said Edo. "Let's be real. It's obvious that Cristiano was dragging the team down, just as these two horses are dragging the carriage."

David nodded.

"He had to go," David said. "Although, I'll always remember him as the greatest player to wear the United shirt. Still, we are better without him."

"So ironic!" said Edo. "As always, he wanted to be the central figure, but with him as the main protagonist at the age of thirty-seven, the team simply didn't work."

"And let's not forget," said David. "Ronaldo revealed some home truths about the Glazers and the way the club does business. So all praise for that!"

"Well," said Edo. "He left just before the World Cup. I believe he wanted to fully focus on his last chance to win *that* trophy. Then, he couldn't return to Europe after the trophy went to Messi's Argentina."

The bus pulled up at traffic lights, and some United fans began banging on the window at the bypassers.

"It hurt him," said David. "Ronaldo wanted that trophy so much. It hurt me as well to watch. I wanted him to win it, too. But Messi wanted it *more*!"

"Messi," said Edo, closing his eyes, then opening them and glancing around at the Victoria train station. "Lionel Messi!"

"I know!" said David, sensing his friend's awe for the player.

"It's difficult to explain the meaning of Messi—his greatness," said Edo.

"Nobody wanted it more than Messi," said David. "The pressure on the man to win the World Cup was beyond reasonable."

Edo nodded.

"You see," he said. "Messi has all Cristiano's striving, needing and wanting—hunger!"

"Yes," said David. "They are *both* obsessed with winning."

"But then Messi has something else as well," said Edo. "He has the touch which cannot be learnt, regardless of how much time or mental effort is invested. He has the touch that comes from *beyond* time and mind. It's a divine gift Ronaldinho awoke in him while they played together in Barcelona. For five years, Messi was basking in the radiant source of all inspiration—Ronaldinho. It made him what he is today."

"Ronaldinho was his mentor, indeed," said David.

"Yes," said Edo. "And he considered him such. Since Messi joined the first team, Ronaldinho made it his mission to watch over him. Do you remember Messi's first goal for Barcelona in La Liga, David?"

"I do," said David. "It was against Albacete in 2005."

"Exactly," said Edo. "Messi was just seventeen. Ronaldinho chipped the ball to Messi in his signature way, and Messi lobbed the keeper beautifully. That combination for the goal between them was sensational, but the real magic was released as they started celebrating the goal. Ronaldinho approached Messi, turned his back and let Messi jump on him. It was like the football gods came together that day—as if something truly remarkable had come to life. Then, other players came, hugged, and started jumping together. Can you imagine, man? They were jumping around like headless rabbits—all smiling like little kids. It looked so stupid. But no, they were leaping because they were celebrating *football*—the essence of football. Then, the fans were also jumping, going wild, unaware that they just witnessed something special. It wasn't long before the Camp Nou faithful started singing *Messi, Messi* chants. The game!"

"The *game*," David muttered, nodding.

"Ronaldinho once said that even when Messi was young, he could see that he was a great player," said Edo. "*When I saw him for the first time, I could see his amazing quality. I didn't teach him anything—he had enough quality himself.*[44] So you see, David, Ronaldinho woke up something deep in Messi that was already there, ready to shine. Messi's divinity comes from that miraculous source, while Cristiano's divinity comes from his ego—from *rejection*."

"Correct me if I'm wrong, but didn't Messi also have to deal with rejection," said David, just as the bus pulled undercover. "His growth hormone disorder was his rejection."

"Yeah, you're right," said Edo. "He did have to deal with rejection. The environment is often cruel to weaker kids, so he had to find a way to persevere. Being the smallest kid in the class and on the football pitch made him develop some resistance. And Lionel's grandma, to whom he still dedicates every goal by pointing to the sky, was his protector."

"Oh, is *that* what his goal celebration is about?" David said. "I didn't know that."

"She used to be his biggest support," said Edo. "Although he was smaller than the others, she always convinced coaches to let Leo play. She knew he possessed the magic that transcended physical disadvantage. And he would come on the pitch and dribble past every player before scoring."

"He was *different*," said David.

"But yeah," said Edo. "There are similarities between Cristiano and Messi in creating the ego based on the urge to *prove* and *protect*. And Messi might have come to Barcelona with that as well. Still, there was a huge difference between the two of them. Messi doesn't play to be the best. Sure, he has needs, wants and a hunger for victory, but no image *depends* on that winning—no personal structures to feed. He's in touch with oneness, so his ego has broader meaning. His ego serves the creation of something way bigger than, perhaps, a personal brand. It serves *football*."

"It serves *life* therefore," said David, softly.

"Indeed," said Edo.

The pair sat in silence for a moment.

"All the mockery stopped when Leo put his football boots on," said Edo. "At that moment, he became *Grande Leo*. That's how his peers would refer to him when he got the ball. And even if the idea of *simply playing* got lost somewhere between his trauma and proving himself, Ronaldinho waited for him at

Barcelona to help revive Messi's inner absoluteness, which never requires any proof and which we all carry but are not all open to."

"Yeah, it takes digging to get there," said David. "A *lot* of digging."

Edo nodded.

"Supposedly—" said Edo. "When a doctor told Messi he had a disorder, his only question was, *Will I be able to play football?*"[45]

"I get all that, my friend," said David. "But how is that any different to Ronaldo, whose only love was football as well—who spent thousands of hours in the streets of Madeira crafting his skills and who appreciated tricks more than anything when it came to football?"

"People already saw Messi as an unprecedented talent at eleven years old," said Edo. "But that wasn't talent, but football itself, in the form of a man."

"They also saw Ronaldo as an unprecedented talent at eleven," said David.

The bus stopped, and the first rows of fans started pouring off.

"Kike Domínguez was a man who coached Messi as a kid at Newell's Old Boys," said Edo, reaching under the seat to grab his bag. "On one occasion, he said that he believed Messi's parents played a great role in helping him reach his true power. He said, *Knowing his parents, I don't think they ever demanded that he be like this or that—his father Jorge was all-natural.*"

"What do you mean, all-natural?" said David, standing up. "As in, Que sera, sera? Whatever will be, will be?"

"Yeah, I guess so," said Edo as they shuffled their way to the front of the bus. "You see, Leo wasn't weighed down with ideas of what he should be or when and why. Only by following your own path can you discover your true power. It seems like every single piece has come together when it comes to Messi and the people around him—his grandma, parents, coaches in Argentina, coaches in Barcelona, teammates, Ronaldinho, Xavi. They *all* played a huge role in what Messi is today."

"Of course," said David as they climbed down the steps and headed toward the tube station. "So many things need to be in place for somebody to become one of the greatest players ever."

"Indeed," said Edo. "The pinnacle of the support for Messi through the years was Pep Guardiola, a man who is a genius himself and who gave Messi freedom in his team. Messi was the first and the last player with absolute freedom in Pep's perfect system."

"Yes!" said David. "I'll never forget when he scored four amazing goals against Arsenal in 2010. It's difficult to say which was better—a long-range shot, one of two chips over the keeper or one through the keeper's legs. That was peak Messi, without a doubt. Pep gave him the full freedom to express himself."

"Absolutely," said Edo. "And such creation can only come from that secret place where there are no losses, no victories and no good or bad—from the place of *no proving*, the Ronaldinho state of mind, the realm of *pure creation*."

"Okay, my friend," said David. "But Gerard *Piqué* once said that Messi was unbearable when he lost. Isn't that the same thing that we talked about with Ronaldo? You know—learning, lessons, defeats, wins, coming back stronger every time and all that?"

Edo thought for a moment.

"Yeah, it's the same," he said. "It's the type of ego they both have and without which, they wouldn't be two of the best players. It's the fear of losing. However, the only thing Messi was afraid to lose along the way was football—not his pride, career, or friends. We could say that Messi is a balance between Ronaldo and Ronaldinho. He carries both Cristiano's rejection and Ronaldinho's acceptance."

"Come on Edo," said David. "That's a bit of a stretch, don't you think?"

"Listen to me," said Edo. "The moment Messi won the World Cup with Argentina—as Montiel was lining up to take the decisive penalty in the shootout, Messi looked at the sky and said: *Puede ser hoy, abu—It could be today, grandma.*[46]

David raised his eyebrows.

"Que sera, sera," he said solemnly. "Whatever will be, will be."

"Seconds later, Argentinian players were crying," said Edo. "And French players were sobbing like children. The coaches, including Lionel Scaloni, were crying. Journalists were crying. Fans were crying. They were all *honoured* to see Messi lift that trophy. And the only person who seemed calmer than the others was—Messi. He *knew* it was coming, just like the rest of us, who had opened the door and made space for Messi's magic in our lives."

"As if some things were destined," said David, looking at the sky.

"To master life," Edo announced, holding up a finger. "Is to find a balance between ego and oneness—between Ronaldo and Ronaldinho."

"Right," said David as they sat on a train to Wembley. "And you think you would find that in Messi?"

Survival Coloured With Fine Art

Dying for Others

David and Edo gazed up the famous Wembley Way, now packed with vast numbers of red shirts scattered like tiny ants gradually getting swallowed by the gigantic Wembley arch.

Hopeful clouds hung above the stadium, painting everything in its overcast, murky light.

David fitted well into the crowd in his deep red Manchester United sweater and a look of hope which matched the clouds. Edo had dressed for warmth in a thick purple fluffy hat, a thick blue scarf, and a brown jacket.

We've seen it all, we've won the lot, we're Man United, and we are never gonna stop, the fans sang as they left the station. *Ole ole, ole ola.*

"It's twelve years since Messi conquered this stadium and won the Champions League against Man United," Edo said, rubbing his nose, which had turned red from the cold.

"Yeah," said David grimly, pulling his red scarf tighter. "Thanks for bringing that up, mate."

"The balance," Edo said. "The balance is where you get to know your purpose. That's when you understand what you are made *of* and what you are made *for*."

"Purpose?" David said. "What is my purpose? Is my purpose to support Man United?"

Edo thought for a moment.

"Hmm," said Edo, mulling it over. "I believe that's probably the role you play."

"The role of a Manchester United supporter," said David. "Doesn't sound too bad."

"Indeed," said Edo, nodding. "And a purpose shows up when you find a balance between that role and the inexplicable vision beyond that role—the vision that comes from the Ronaldinho state of mind. Do you know what I mean, David?"

"Not really," said David, scratching his head.

"It's the balance between love for the badge and love itself," said Edo.

"Which love?" said David.

"Simply love," said Edo. "The one that everything comes from—t*hat* love—love of life—love of football. Only when you love fully can you create in the way Messi creates. Only then can you let the river of inspiration flow through you."

"Check it out," David muttered as thousands of Newcastle fans joined the march towards the stadium.

"Just look at Messi," said Edo. "He dies for his club every weekend and suffers for his country immensely. But since he carries Ronaldinho's oneness, the source of all love, it's not all about him. It's never been about him. It's about the people—about football. He dies for *them*."

"It's no wonder Argentinian fans bow down every time he gets the ball," said David, bowing as he said it.

"Exactly!" said Edo. "The connection between Messi and Argentinian fans is beyond rational. And it can only be that way because Messi is giving himself *fully*. When you align with your purpose, you align with the universe. Life unfolds in the most spectacular ways for everyone involved."

David nodded.

"So if I use my *Manchester United role* to serve the community, is that my purpose then?" he said.

"Kind of," said Edo. "But it can't be about *you.* It can't be about you finding meaning in that or becoming better and more complete. It has to come from the state of consciousness where you are already complete—where you are life itself. Only then are you capable of giving unconditionally. In any other way, it will be about ego—about proving something."

"I *think* I understand," said David as a group of Newcastle fans started singing loudly.

"It's like having a bakery and making beautiful Shepherd's loaves," said Edo. "But at the same time, teaching Arafat to make the same quality of bread—and not being stingy on that one special ingredient—*love.*"

David smiled.

"I like that, my friend," he said. "All in the name of community—so people can eat good bread, right?"

"Indeed," said Edo. "It's when you and your bakery continue to grow through defeats, but deep down, you are always complete nonetheless."

"Yeah," said David. "Messi gave Barcelona and Argentinian fans some very good bread."

"They see him as a god," said Edo. "Or, rather, a *Greek* god—with all the human attributes as well."

"Right," said David. "Because Messi dies to deliver during every game. It means the world when he scores. It's as simple as that—lack of compassion and big ego, remember?"

"Yeah, it's just a question of what you're scoring in the name of," said Edo.

"Right," said David, patting his friend on the back.

"Messi dwells in the fine balance between survival and the beautiful game of football," said Edo. "He resides in the space between inflicting pain on others and having all-comprehensive love for the whole of the game. Messi is life to its *fullest*—life fulfilled with raw, animalistic instincts and immense art and creativity known only to those who have already died in a way."

"Life to the fullest," David mumbled, stretching up to get a better look at the Newcastle fans.

"On one occasion," Edo continued. "Pep was giving a motivational speech to his Manchester City players, and he screamed, *Do you know why Messi is the best player I have ever seen? Because he is a competitor. He is an animal.*"[47]

"A *different* kind of animal, though!" said David.

"Absolutely," said Edo. "And Pep didn't *need* to tell them Messi was an artist because it was obvious. But he did need to explain Messi's killer instinct to them—Messi's *Cristiano* nature!"

"Balance," David said, taking a deep, anticipatory breath.

The pair approached the great stadium and looked up at the famous Wembley arch that flexed and stretched from one side of the arena to the other as if it was holding the whole thing together.

"Balance," said Edo, pointing up at the arch. "Just focus, creativity and skills that are inexplicable, as we have seen so many times from Messi."

"Yes, my friend," said David. "And suffering!"

"Yes," said Edo. "Suffering, but a *different* kind of suffering."

"Oh yeah?"

"Yeah. No acting, no diving."

"No diving?" David barked as the adrenaline started to surge through his body.

"Have you ever seen Messi dive?" Edo asked.

David thought for a moment.

"I don't think so," he said. "I don't remember being pissed off with him, even during the *peak diving years*."

"That's because he never dives," said Edo. "Even when there's an obvious foul made on him, he tries to stay on his feet and make it count. Someone so genuine does not need to play the victim—does not need to limit themselves to useless roles. His opponents assaulted him for the last twenty years, but he has dodged the danger with dignity ever since."

"Oh, that goal he scored when he was nineteen against Getafe—when he embodied the spirit of Maradona," said David, raising his voice to get above the growing crowd.

"Precisely!" said Edo.

David started waving his hands around, describing the action.

"Messi got the ball in the Getafe half, dodged one tackle, then nutmegged another player instinctively, without even seeing him come from the side."

"I know," said Edo. "He just passed through them like a ghost. It's the balance between creativity and absolute ruthlessness driven by an attacking mindset. The defender he nutmegged tried to recover, and he tracked Messi back to the box where another two players waited. But not one of them could stop him. He sold them a couple of tricks and laid them down on the grass as if they were wooden dolls."

"He was gone, leaving them all for dust!" shouted David, raising his fists. "With only the goalie to beat, Messi faked a shot, confusing the keeper. Then he weaved and hit the ball with his weaker right foot. The Getafe right back came screaming in from nowhere and attempted to clear the ball off the line, but the ball hit the back of the net."

"Incomprehensible!" said Edo, shaking his head as the pair approached the security control at the stadium. "Every *player* tried to put him down—each one a potential foul. And if he were a different type of player, Messi would have gone down on the first tackle to win the free kick. But he kept going until they were all left sunbathing on the grass, including the keeper, who went for the final tackle. None of them stood a chance of getting Messi out of that run."

"Yeah," shouted David, whose excitement was getting out of control.

"And you can't say the same for Cristiano," said Edo. "He's always been prone to diving here and there."

"Oh, come on!" said David. "He's changed, Edo! Sure, he was a diver at the start of his career. But as he matured, he stopped. Also, you need to remember that he was moving at such an unnaturally high speed that every little touch would kick him out of balance."

“And Messi was *not* moving at an unnaturally high speed?” said Edo.

“Yes,” said David. “But Messi has a low centre of gravity.”

“Exactly,” said Edo, holding up a finger. “Because *balance* is permeating his entire being.”

Observing the Moment

When Time Stops

Excited fans had packed Wembley to capacity—half Manchester United, half Newcastle, sliced perfectly down the centre.

David and Edo shuffled toward their seats among the United supporters, high up in the stand with a good view of the stadium.

"What a perfect balance this is," said Edo. "Half red and half black and white—just *perfectly* balanced."

David was visibly enjoying himself as they took their seats among the red supporters.

"Messi is *always* a step ahead of everybody else," Edo said. "While others make a single move, Messi makes two. Some Barcelona people confessed that when he first arrived, he would always stay in the corner of the dressing room, observing others, and that only then would he be at ease."

"Oh yeah?" said David.

"Also, when a match starts," Edo continued. "You often see him not moving much, just strolling around for the first couple of minutes—observing the moment. And that's when you know—he *is* football."

"Okay," said David, listening with one ear while absorbing the atmosphere at the stadium. "I've got goosebumps, my friend. This is *astonishing*."

"Only when you are absolutely focused on the present moment can you reach your true self and, therefore, your true power, David," said Edo. "And the other way around, too. Only when you reach your true self can you fully focus on the present moment. Because when you reach that point, you don't need to prove anything to anyone anymore. You are complete. Whereas ego seeks meaning in the future, as in *I will be the best when I do that and that*."

"Right," said David.

"But when you connect to your true self," Edo continued. "And you realise you are complete already. You cease to look for meaning in the future or past. Therefore, on the opposite side of ego dwells the present moment where one is liberated from that burden of ego—from proving something. One can observe the present moment and see things for what they are without subjective perspectives. And they who see things as they are, see *more*, David. Those people can truly observe."

"I feel present at the moment," said David. "I am fully immersed in my passion for Man United."

"Indeed," said Edo. "But a true observer doesn't need to add mental concepts to what they see. There is no identification when it comes to true observance—no Manchester United nor Newcastle. A true observer sees with *no* subjective perceptions."

"How is that possible?" said David. "I'd like to learn that."

"Well," said Edo. "Ironically, it's here for you right now. And for everybody else who can detach themselves from the game's laws and observe them from a distance, rather than identifying with them."

David didn't say anything.

Edo turned toward his friend.

"If you are feeling part of the Man United group, David, you are observing the situation through the lens of the *past*. The emotions you are experiencing are based on your identification, which only exists due to past experiences you had as a Man United fan."

David screwed up his nose.

"So I need to forget about my past and future?" he said.

"Sort of," said Edo. "Not *forget as such* but see them for what they are—just thoughts. The mind only exists in time. It's essentially about de-identifying with your egoic mind, David. Once a person gets there and realises that they are not their mind, they get a unique opportunity to control the mind instead of being controlled by it. At that point, a person gains limitless power and the ability to use their mind as a tool. They stop *being* their mind. That's when extra space opens up, and they start seeing clearer."

"Interesting," said David.

"You become more *aware* of things around you and also aware of your mind," continued Edo.

"What do you mean aware, Edo?" said David.

Edo shuffled forward on his chair.

"Aware of the role you play, David," he said. "Aware of your mind—your ego. And ultimately aware that you are *not* your ego. To be aware is to be uncontrolled by that, but to be able to control that instead—to be able to control t*he role you play*."

"And that's why Messi is always a step ahead?" said David.

They stood up to let a group pass.

"Robert Moreno, the former manager of Spain," said Edo, leaning into David's ear. "He spent three years as assistant manager at Barcelona and said once that Messi plays a different game to everybody else. *You can't train him. He is football. With*

Leo, it's like the Matrix. He can see the movement of the legs of the opponent, and he sees the movement of the goalkeepers and has the ability to react.[48] You see, David, only when you are truly present can you unlock such power. Only then can you escape the Matrix—the conditioned personal and social systems."

"Okay, that's good," said David, sitting back down.

Edo sat down as well.

"It's the *balance* between Ronaldinho's acceptance of what he is and Cristiano's refusal to be content with what he has," Edo said. "I guess *that's* when you can more easily accept the things you don't have control over and focus more on the things you do. In the balance, you've got all the tools to maximise your potential."

David stared over at the Newcastle end, who were clapping their team, now warming up on the field.

"Remember that goal Messi scored against Real Madrid in the 2011 Champions League semi-final?" he said. "That goal was so special, my friend."

"Oh, yes!" said Edo, placing his hands together.

David took up his usual aggressive stance.

"The rivalry between Real and Barca was at its peak," he said. "And that game was the boiling point. It was a historic battle in a war that had long been out of control during the season when Barcelona whipped Mourinho 5-0, and Pep and Mourinho became fierce enemies. Pep, in the press conference before that semi-final, even called Mourinho *el puto jefe*, saying that he was the *fucking master* in the press conference room and that José had won every single battle *off* the pitch that season."[49]

"Yeah," said Edo, nodding. "Pep couldn't deal with the constant provocations anymore. He finally lost it before that semi-final and challenged Mourinho on the pitch."

"Mou dragged Pep into his world!" yelled David, punching the air. "Mou *did* win the battle in the press conference room if he managed to get Pep swearing at him in front of the media. Well done, Mou."

"Well," said Edo. "The game was a clash of two worlds—two philosophies so far from each other that they almost met at the same point. It was Spain versus Catalonia, Madrid versus Barcelona, Pep versus Mourinho, attacking versus defensive football. It was the *perfect* balance. It was Real Madrid against, probably, the strongest team that ever played the game."

"It was Xavi, Iniesta and Messi against Lass Diarra, Xabi Alonso and Pepe," David said, punching the air again. "Mou went all in *Mou* and put Pepe in the midfield to get another destructor of the game."

"Typical," said Edo.

"The game was so ugly, though," said David. "It was full of theatrics and faking. Barcelona were unbearable to watch, exaggerating every single tackle."

"And, let's be honest, *the destructors* kept kicking them," said Edo. "Mourinho ordered war, and he got war. His players held their positions firmly. Santiago Bernabéu was waiting for a miracle, for just one counterattack—for Xabi Alonso to release Cristiano and get them something out of the game."

"And then Pepe got the straight red card for a tackle on Dani Alves!" said David.

"Yep," said Edo. "A small personal victory for Mourinho, who blamed referees, saying they had been helping Barcelona the whole season.[50] It was a game of cynicism and mockery."

"Mourinho was right, if you ask me," said David. "That was the fourth El Clásico that season and all of them ended with Madrid having ten men in the field."

"Anyway," said Edo. "Madrid could only defend from that point, but it wasn't enough when Messi attacked a cross in the box and put the ball in the net."

"The guy was ruthless," said David.

Edo nodded enthusiastically.

"Ruthless!" he said. "The game was drawing to a close, and Real were defending a man short, hoping they could make it to the second leg only 1-0 down. Two systems were clashing hard. The atmosphere was tense. The players and fans were on a knife edge. The cities of Madrid and Barcelona were restless. Ronaldo was furious. Mourinho was praying to the heavens and arguing with referees. Real players kept kicking Barcelona players. Barcelona kept exaggerating the pain. It was chaos. But then—"

"Then?" said David, grinning.

"Then the *eighty-seventh minute* happened," said Edo, standing above his friend. "Time stopped as if the moon had flipped over, illuminating Santiago *Bernabéu*, making badges unrecognisable and both teams' shirts pale. So for a moment, there was no difference between the teams. The fans went silent, and the rivalry dissolved. Pep and Mou saw God. For one second, Xabi Alonso and Lass Diarra couldn't agree who was taking Messi, and that was enough for him to pass through in between them. He passed the first wall of defence, gained momentum, and slipped by the rest of the defenders for a laugh—Ramos, Arbeloa, Marcelo—one, two, three. They couldn't get near him. And then a right-footed shot—"

"Time stopped." whispered David.

"All the concepts disappeared," said Edo.

They both felt the great silence seeping in from the memory of that great night and penetrating Wembley stadium at that moment, where they both stood among almost ninety thousand football fans.

"That was it," said Edo. "Madrid's dream of making the Champions League final was finished. And Mourinho's Real Madrid dream was gone."

"Surreal," said David.

"And you know what?" said Edo. "*Years* later, Xabi Alonso said that Mourinho, Ramos and himself had spent hours trying to devise a plan to stop Messi.[51] But Messi was more present than them. He was more aware."

Focus on Diversity

Lighter Than the Future

The stadium almost shook from its foundations as the final trumpets of *God Save The King* gave way to a deafening roar from the fans.

"Alright, guys," yelled David, clapping his hands and rubbing his palms together. "Let's *focus* and bring home the first trophy after six long years of drought."

"*Focus,*" Edo shouted as the roar died down into applause. "It's funny that you mention it."

"Yeah, *focus*," David said, chewing on gum manically and tapping his leg like someone nervously waiting for important news.

"Focus is extremely important," said Edo. "For whatever you want to achieve in life."

"It must be," said David, who was always impressed with his friend's ability to speak with composure through all events.

"And it comes from being *present*," said Edo.

"*Let's go*, boys," David shouted alongside another deafening roar as the referee blew the whistle and United kicked off.

"When you are focused, you have everything you need to create your own miracles," shouted Edo. "Small or big miracles—it doesn't matter. When you are focused, every game is a miracle."

"You know," said David, leaning into his friend while keeping his eyes fixed on the game. "Whenever a journalist asks a manager if their team can reach the final of the Champions

League or perhaps win a domestic title, they *always* answer, *We're just focusing on the next match. The next match is our final.*"

"True," said Edo. "They *always* say that."

"It seems as if managers have figured out the importance of focus then," said David.

Edo thought for a moment.

"Yeah, I guess some of them understand that their players need to be focused on the next match if they want to stand a chance," he said. "If they get lost in their minds and thoughts about the future, then they can't be fully present—fully *focused*. Focus is the result of taking away the burden of the future. Focus is the result of living in the *present*. And you might not believe it, but the present will bring you a better future than you could ever dream of. It will get you into the final and bring you the trophies."

"Man United must have been doing quite a good job with it then," said David.

"I think Claudio Ranieri got that one right—in terms of focus," said Edo. "How else can you explain the 2015/16 season and what Leicester achieved with him as a manager?"

"That season is *still* unexplainable," said David, swinging his arms theatrically. "It's the greatest story in football history if you ask me. Leicester to win the Premier League ten points clear in the competition with Arsenal, Tottenham, Manchester City, Manchester United, Liverpool, Chelsea? Who could have dreamt that up?"

"It was truly incredible!" Edo said, nodding enthusiastically.

"And," said David. "It's a note that sticks out in the history of football serving as a great reminder of why we don't need the

Super League. As Marcelo Bielsa once said, *Football is the most popular sport globally because the weak can beat the powerful.*[52] The Super League would destroy that important premise."

"True," said Edo. "And, yeah, throughout the whole season, we all thought, *Okay, Leicester will collapse soon*. But somehow, they never did. They pushed through to the end."

"It makes no sense," said David. "Only two years earlier, they got promoted to the Premier League, and shortly after, they marginally survived relegation back to the Championship in the most extraordinary way. And *then*, from out of nowhere, they somehow won the toughest league in the world. They *won* it!"

Edo laughed like a maniac.

"Crazy!" he said.

"Many things had to come together, though," said David. "Ranieri claims it was about fighting mentality. Kasper Schmeichel claims it was about togetherness. But I think it was about one thing—Jamie Vardy!"

"Jamie Vardy!" Edo repeated calmly.

"*Fucking* Jamie Vardy!" said David. "His story is similar to the Leicester story. He went from a non-league hero to a record-breaking striker among the best in English football. He scored for the eleventh consecutive match against United to break Van Nistelrooy's goal-scoring streak record."

"That goal against Liverpool, though," said Edo. "When Mahrez sent him a long ball through, Vardy volleyed it from thirty metres out into the top bins without even thinking. That was sheer power right there, man. Vardy was lighter than the future."

"Absolutely," said David. "Vardy epitomised that Leicester squad—resilient, sharp, determined, and above all—loyal.

He *was* Leicester. Unlike other stars, the fact that he didn't leave for a bigger club after that season proved he was more than a regular player. That sounds like love, right, Edo?"

"I suppose," said Edo.

"You see, my friend," said David. "Without such loyalty to a club—without such strong *identification* with the club and the badge, the miracle wouldn't be possible. Without such strong identification with the city and the community, Leicester wouldn't have become the champions."

Edo leaned back in his chair for a moment.

"Interesting that you mention the community," he said. "Because Leicester is one of the most diverse cities in England, making the Leicester fans diverse as well. And funnily enough, that winning team was one of the most international teams ever. For instance, the starting eleven for that game against Liverpool was made up of a Dane, a Jamaican, a German, an Austrian, a Frenchman, an Algerian, a Japanese man and only four Englishmen, most of whom had spent only a couple of years at the club."

"Okay," said David.

"And yet," Edo continued. "The manager was an Italian who insisted that he wanted to create a team based on Italian tactics and English performance."[53]

"Yeah, so why are you telling me that?" said David.

"Because David, *all* of them brought a bit of their identity to that team," said Edo, cheering up. "They all brought different perspectives to the squad, different ways of seeing the world. Often, when so many perspectives come together, a space for growth opens up, and empathy for one another appears. There's no one solid identity that stands out."

David turned away from the game for a moment to face his friend.

"Yes!" he said. "It's like having a bakery where an Italian makes the dough for the bread, a Turk is in charge of the crust, a Croatian brings the spices, an Argentinian brings the corn, and a Frenchman does the presentation in an English bakery."

"I like that," said Edo. "Leicester's club ambassador Alan Birchenall said that the secret of winning the league was a lack of egos in the squad."

David turned back to the game.

"But if there is *no* ego in the squad," he said. "How are they able to win? Don't you remember, Edo? You can't win without ego. You have to make others miserable for you to win."

"Because ego is controlled," said Edo calmly. "And it's used as a *tool*. It doesn't create unnecessary suffering where it doesn't need to. It creates suffering for other teams only—laws of the game, right? When the ego *isn't* under control, it creates suffering for everybody, teammates included."

"So the miracle happens when you control your ego?" said David.

"Yes," said Edo. "That, my dear friend, is the secret of success in football. That's when the team becomes a real unit, and they play as one. Ranieri called it *the team spirit* and claimed it was their best player. Assistant manager Craig Shakespeare said he'd never seen such chemistry between players."

"Wow," said David. "That's very inspiring, mate. I think the one game that will stay with me was against Man City sometime in

February. Leicester beat City 3-1 away from home. I think that was the game when fans started to believe that the impossible could become possible."

"Stunning!" said Edo. "Nicely put, David."

"Thanks," said David. "I don't think even the players believed they could beat City at the Etihad. And then, surprise! Robert Huth, with two goals from set-pieces, and the incredible Mahrez dribbling past a few City defenders and then *bam*!"

"No Jamie Vardy on the scoresheet, though," said Edo.

"No Jamie," said David. "But only the squad with no egos."

"Interesting," said Edo. "Even though they were five points clear of second place Spurs after that match. And even though Leicester still looked mighty, and people started talking about their chances of winning the title, they didn't get distracted. Lack of egos equals present moment, equals focus. Game by game. Until the trophy, David, my friend."

"Wow," said David, clapping as De Gea saved a shot.

"Craig Shakespeare said it was about calmness as well," Edo said. "Calmness is one of the most significant fruits of being present. Leicester weren't distracted for a second. Even when it became obvious they would win it, they only focused on the next match. The only time Ranieri said they were ready to win the league was before the Swansea game in gameweek thirty-five. And even then, the focus remained strong. Ranieri didn't let anybody or anything near the team."

"So impressive," said David. "They were released from the future and past. And throughout the season, he kept assuring them that the result was unimportant, but only their attitudes mattered."

"Absolutely," said Edo. "And eventually, they won it two matches before the end of the season. The celebration *could* begin. And despite the diversity in the city of Leicester, they all gathered and celebrated as one. You see, David, due to the laws of the game, football and society might not yet be ready to lose their egos fully and become Ronaldinho, but bringing different cultures together and allowing different perspectives to mix is a step forward on the path of rising consciousness."

"And creating miracles," said David.

"And spreading empathy," Edo said. "Eventually, empathy will spread across the borders as well."

Calmness in the Blaze of Fire

The Rich Man

The game was coming to an end, and United were 2-0 up against Newcastle in the final of the League Cup.

We'll never die, we'll never die, sang the United fans loudly as the game slipped into injury time.

"It's a miracle!" David screamed, lifting his scarf in the air. "We'll never die, we'll never die, we'll keep the red flag flying high, cos Man United never die!"

"Manchester United winning the League Cup is not quite a miracle," said Edo. "But I'm sure it means a lot for you guys."

"It does!" said David.

"Miracles—the beautiful game has provided quite a few of them," said Edo.

"Life," said David. "*Life*, Edo!"

"Carlo Ancelotti *alone* has provided quite a few of them," said Edo. "His Real Madrid Champions League campaign in 2022 was one great miracle. To this day, I'm still not sure if I can grasp how they won the Champions League last year."

"Yeah," said David, dancing with the United fans. "It *never* looked like it was going to end that way."

"They came back from death multiple times," said Edo. "And I mean *real* death. But no matter how deep they got and how hopeless the situation seemed, they *never* panicked. Ancelotti never panicked. He seemed calm the entire way along."

"Perhaps it's the gum that keeps him calm, Edo?" said David, chewing hard on his own gum. "Although Carlo chews the chewing gum so fiercely, he always seems calm. Such are the ways of the Carlo."

David put his hands together and bowed to an invisible Carlo in the sky.

"Well, they played Paris Saint-Germain in the first knockout round, and they were nowhere near their opponents," said Edo. "For a hundred and fifty minutes, Paris were all over Real and 2-0 up on aggregate. And then, Karim Benzema emerged like he had never emerged before. He punished PSG's mistakes and *ruthlessly* scored three goals in seventeen minutes for a total comeback."

"I know," said David. "It proved that a dystopian club as PSG, with Messi, Neymar, and Mbappé in the same team, can't work."

"Yeah," said Edo. "But seriously, what happened with Benzema that year? Carlo always knew how to get the best out of his players when they needed it the most. So often he pulled something extra from his players that we weren't even aware they possessed."

"He did the same in 2007 when he conquered Europe with AC Milan," said David with a half grimace. "They eliminated us in the semi-finals when Kaká put in the performance to end all performances and scored that epic goal. Do you remember Edo? After he put his head in between Evra and Heinze, they clashed into each other while Kaká slipped through them untouched and scored against Van der Sar."

"I do remember," said Edo. "I loved that goal."

“Kaká won Ballon d’Or later that year,” said David. “He was simply amazing. Ancelotti pulled something extra out of him that year. But not only Kaká, that squad was a *proper* team with all the right characteristics. Every position was rock solid. And more than that.”

“Carlo knew how to exploit everyone’s abilities to the fullest,” Edo interrupted. “He knew the strengths and weaknesses of his players.”

“*Right*,” said David. “And you can only do that if you recognise your players' roles and their roles in the team.”

“Yes!” said Edo. “And more importantly to recognise them primarily as human beings beyond those roles. Take, for instance, Gattuso—as we established last time, a guy with obvious anger issues. It takes a lot of awareness to control such an intense temperament—to make the most of it without allowing it to create too many problems. Sometimes, Gattuso would simply love making drama for everybody.”

“Clearly!” said David.

“But most of the time,” said Edo. “He turned his issues to his favour and used them as a tool to dominate the football pitch. And the secret, David, is to be *aware* of your emotions and thoughts. That’s when people can use their anger as a tool rather than allowing it to consume them. And *that’s* where they find the balance.”

“Yes,” said David, visibly excited as the United fans whistled, desperate for the game to end.

“Carlo’s role was crucial there,” shouted Edo, determined to finish the conversation over the howls. “*He* was the one who truly understood Gattuso and who let him be himself.”

"Yes, my friend. And in return, Carlo got a warrior like no other," shouted David. "Carlo knew how to exploit Gattuso's role."

"It makes sense!" said Edo.

"*Of course*, it makes sense, my friend," David said proudly, now drunk on the impending victory. "Just as Carlo knew how to exploit Luka Modrić's role in 2022."

"Right," said Edo.

"What an *unbelievable* assist Modrić provided for Rodrygo in the second game of the quarter-finals against Chelsea," David yelled. "Benzema scored yet another hat-trick in the first leg, and now it was Real who were 3-0 down with Chelsea seeming almost guaranteed to go through. Then, Real got their shit together, took the game to extra time where Benz finished the job."

"Of course," said Edo. "It was Benzema *again*—a well-deserved Ballon d'Or! Isn't it interesting how he only blossomed when Cristiano left Madrid? In Carlo's first spell at the club, it was *all* about Cristiano. Everybody was there to serve Ronaldo, and Benzema was there to assist him."

"And Benzema was executing that role brilliantly, too," said David. "He *knew* his place in the team."

"True!" said Edo.

"That's the real magic of Carlo Ancelotti," said David. "He *knew* how to balance everyone's needs into the team. And that's when you can also find a balance between defence and attack—the balance sought by every manager."

"Yes, *balance,*" said Edo.

"Ronaldo loved Ancelotti because he let him play in his favourite position as a left winger rather than a striker," said David. "Ronaldo believed he was the strongest there, so Ancelotti said, *Okay*."

"And that approach attracted many of the best players," said Edo. "Do you know, David, that Carlo coached *ten* Ballon d'Or winners in his career?"

"Ten?" said David, spinning briefly toward Edo. "How is that even possible?"

Edo cleared his throat.

"Cannavaro, Zidane, Rivaldo, Shevchenko, Fat Ronaldo, Ronaldinho, Kaká, Cristiano, Modrić and Benzema," Edo spun off proudly.

"That's beyond imagination," said David. "How come no one talks about that?"

"Not sure," said Edo. "But it's an insane statistic. And Carlo must be an unbelievably rich man. That means he had an opportunity to learn about football from *all* of them. Just *imagine* what it's like to take a piece of football from each one—a piece from Cristiano, a piece from Ronaldinho and so on."

"You see, Carlo never had a problem with Ronaldo's personality," shouted David. "Ronaldo never gave him any problems. On the contrary. Ancelotti once said about Ronaldo, *He solved my problems*.[54] After all, they won the Champions League together in 2014—a trophy Carlo ranks among his favourite titles.[55] Then again, Ronaldinho and Carlo weren't exactly best friends. But Ronaldinho only joined Carlo when Ronaldinho started to decline."

"Started to decline as a professional football player, you mean?" snapped Edo.

"What?" said David.

"Ronaldinho only declined as a professional football player," said Edo. "Football itself never declined in Ronaldinho."

"Right," said David.

"And then the semi-finals against Man City arrived for Real Madrid," said Edo. "God knows how they survived that. They were 5-3 down in the ninetieth minute of the second leg. Madrid were shotless for the whole match—nothing. They were burning up in a blaze of City fire. And then Rodrygo scored two in two minutes to take the game to extra time."

"Unbelievable!" said David.

"How did they survive that?" Edo asked. "How? And the craziest thing was that Modrić, Kroos and Casemiro—the *team's backbone*—were all on the bench while several youngsters were out there making that miracle happen."

"Their role was crucial that day," said David. "Carlo struck just the right balance between young and old players."

"One player who was still on the pitch, of course, was Karim Benzema," said Edo. "The man was awarded a penalty in extra time and sent it home brilliantly! And Carlo was *calm* again. Even though the players were burning on the inside, they *needed* Carlo's calm to stop them from burning out. It seemed like Carlo always knew *everything* was possible in football."

"He just lifts his eyebrow, and the magic happens," said David, waving his fists around in desperation for the final whistle.

"He finally lost his calm, shedding a few tears after the final whistle," said Edo.

David's eyes filled with tears as Edo smiled at his friend.

"You're nearly there," said Edo. "And for Carlo, that final against Liverpool in Paris was not there to lose after everything they had been through. 1-0 was enough for the title."

"Remarkable," said David, looking emotional. "Carlo struck the balance between attack and defence just right in that one."

"Yeah, he has struck quite a few balances well," said Edo.

"That was his *fourth* Champions League title," David shouted, trying to get above the crazy whistles. "Nobody has more than him. Ancelotti conquered the whole of Europe. He is the *only* one to win the title in all five major European leagues. He triumphed in Italy with Milan, in England with Chelsea, in France with Paris, in Germany with Bayern and in Spain with Real Madrid."

"His calm might be the product of that," Edo shouted. "At least partially."

"A product of what?" said David.

"Of seeing different perspectives," shouted Edo. "Living and coaching in different countries, exposing himself to uncertainties, to the zone of discomfort."

"Right—" said David. "Where one learns excessively and moves through life like an optimist, *ready* for the new challenges. He grows through life! But isn't that life with *no* peace, rather than life with peace and calm?"

"It might be the turbulent life with turbulent events," yelled Edo over the whistles. "But when a person gets exposed to the uncertainties so much, they already know that life will turn out well, one way or another. And *that* gives you the strength to accept, which brings you peace—the *true* peace from within. Only when the mind is peaceful and still can true change happen. Even in stoppage time when all seems lost, David."

The referee blew a long blast on his whistle, and the United fans erupted, dancing and screaming and singing.

"That's it," shouted David, jumping up and down. "The trophy is *ours*! Glory, glory, Man United, Glory, glory, Man United, Glory, glory, Man United and the Reds go marching *on on on*."

Edo smiled at his friend, then faced the pitch and clapped his usual conservative clap.

The Champion of the World

Football Has Won

The League Cup winner's ceremony was ending, and the stadium was gradually emptying. After they lifted the trophy in the stands of Wembley, the United players did it one more time on the pitch, and only the most loyal fans stayed to see it for a second time.

David and Edo came from their seats to stand pitchside for the festivities.

"The only person missing on the list of players Carlo Ancelotti has coached is Leo Messi," said Edo. "But that would be a bit too much, even for Carlo!"

"Yeah," said David with bitterness in his voice. "Messi is stuck in that dystopian club at the moment. Paris Saint-Germain is proof that money can't buy a team. I mean, Messi, Neymar and Mbappé artificially planted in the same squad—is that football? Is that passion? Paris Saint-Germain? Seriously?"

"I hear you," said Edo, squinting at the players dancing on the pitch.

"From the first day Messi joined the club, there's always been some drama around that team," said David. "Too much ego in one club."

"Well, you're not wrong," said Edo.

"Not once has Mbappé signalled he wanted to leave the club," David said. "And although Messi and Mbappé found some peace and later praised each other publicly, there's always been something *off*."[56]

"The results speak for themselves, man," said Edo. "They've won *nothing* significant since Messi joined. They couldn't even win the French Cup in two attempts! It's true, they won the French league title, but they could have done it without Messi just as easily as they have done *most* of the time. They brought Messi in for the Champions League! But it's not happening. They *certainly* won't win the Champions League this year, either. They're 1-0 down against Bayern, and they play the second leg in ten days in Munich. I'm *sure* they're going out."

"How to explain *that* paradox?" said David as he watched his team gather around the trophy.

"The moment Kylian Mbappé had his first doubt about playing alongside Messi was when he said *no* to football," said Edo. "He said no to the *purest* of football—to life. Because Messi *is* football—a stream of all-comprehensive footballing intelligence, who sees the game differently, and he understands it differently. Only the lucky few get a chance to share the dressing room with Messi. And the ones who have allowed that intelligence into their lives have been transformed forever. Iniesta and Xavi touched that source and became history's most creative midfield duo. Luis Suárez drunk from the well and gained some ridiculous vision of moving in between lines. Sergio Busquets figured out the point of football, while Dani Alves even danced on the pitch."

"*There* we go!" David said, clenching his fists as Bruno Fernandes and Harry Maguire lifted the trophy just before David and Edo. "*Yeah!*"

The United players sprayed champagne and chased each other around the pitch.

"It's the same intelligence Messi inherited from Ronaldinho," Edo said. "Only the chosen ones had the opportunity to make contact with it. It's an intelligence so powerful that it breaks down all the illusions players have of themselves. It opens their eyes to *true* football."

David kept clapping and staring at the United players.

"Yet, here we are," said Edo. "Mbappé is proof that not every rock can be turned into gold—at least not overnight anyway."

"Well, that's fascinating," said David.

"The universe sent a gift to Mbappé, and he said no—*I am bigger than football. I am bigger than life,"* said Edo.

"Neymar, on the other hand, let Messi in!" said David.

"Indeed," said Edo. "Ronaldinho once said that just as he had helped Messi, he was sure Messi would help Neymar.[57] Brazilians or Argentinians—it didn't matter. They were all the same there."

"That's why Neymar was happy when Messi joined them in Paris," David said. "He knew that *football* was coming."

"They had some *great* days in Barcelona," said Edo as the pair turned around and walked back up the stairs towards the exit. "But it wasn't all that bright when Neymar first joined Barca. He said that in the beginning, he couldn't feel himself. *The pressure and expectations were pulling me down. However, after a talk I had with Messi, it all changed. I started feeling lighter.*"[58]

"Lighter than the future, perhaps!" said David.

"Messi won his last Champions League in 2015 alongside Neymar," said Edo. "What a team that was—Messi, Neymar, Suárez."

"Pretty similar to the current one in Paris, really," said David. "They were just gathered differently and in different circumstances."

"Yeah," said Edo, looking surprised. "Who could have guessed that would be Messi's last Champions League trophy!"

"He *did* win the World Cup eventually instead, my friend," said David, smiling.

"And what a World Cup he had," said Edo.

"Simply out of this world," said David. "He got *man of the match* five times on Argentina's journey. For me, it became clear Messi meant business in the semi against mighty Croatia, who had just beaten Brazil and believed they could go all the way this time. That's the game when I realised it might have been in the stars for Messi and Argentina."

"The third Argentinian goal was *memorable*," said Edo.

"So memorable," said David, gently punching Edo on the shoulder. "Correct me if I'm wrong, Edo, but Messi was playing one of the last great matches of his life. He had some pain in his left hamstring and kept checking his leg for the whole game, massaging it occasionally. Then, shortly past the hour mark, Lionel Messi, aged *thirty-five*, got the ball in the centre of the pitch and sprinted towards the Croatian goal, racing with Joško Gvardiol, one of the best young centre-backs in the world. And Gvardiol, by the way, had been compared to Virgil van Dijk at that point. Anyway, Gvardiol managed to track Messi and close down the space towards the goal before Messi took another run. The defender tracked Messi again, leaving him isolated on the side of the box. Gvardiol thought he had Messi as the Argentinian turned his back to goal and returned towards the opposite side before opening up onto his injured left foot."

"His *mythological* left foot," said Edo.

"Indeed," said David, pointing at Edo. "Messi sold the fake and went onto his right foot instead, drove towards the corner line, getting just a foot in front of Gvardiol, opening himself up a tiny path to goal. Then, from five metres, he passed diagonally to Julián Álvarez to make it 3-0."

The pair stopped at the top of the steps, looking at the great Wembley stadium and the United players disappearing back toward the dressing rooms.

David took a deep breath.

"The eruption of joy by the Argentinian fans almost broke the stadium," he said.

"What a World Cup that was!" said Edo. "But you see, David, you enjoyed it, but that World Cup was the same as PSG. The people who turned Paris Saint-Germain into a dystopian club are the same Qatari people who organised that tournament. They used the same financial sources for both. The same owners made the decisions."

"Yeah, that's true," said David. "But let's not forget that PSG *didn't* participate in the Super League project. And everything is better than the Super League. We must give them *some* credit at the end of the day."

"PSG was *not* part of the Super League project, no," Edo said. "But *not* because of the nature of the club, but because they had an interest in some other projects which were equally as unromantic. From my point of view, this World Cup in Qatar, which was compromised by who-knows-what is essentially not very different from the Super League. And you said there wouldn't be any passion left in the case of the Super League."

"I did," said David.

"Is this passion, though?" said Edo. "The World Cup in Qatar—the country that barely knows football? Is that passion?"

"It's *still* a World Cup," said David. "With people who love football—with players who love their countries—with some new, fresh players and some time-worn legends who have been around for twenty years."

"Sure," said Edo. "But I'm just saying that money controls the game on every level, pal. The Super League is simply a logical continuation of events, just as the World Cup in Qatar is—*and* Paris Saint-Germain."

"Edo, we can't deny that Messi winning the World Cup was romantic! Sure, everything about that World Cup was weird, but in the end, we saw some *real* beauty."

"No, we can't deny that," Edo admitted. "But that only shows us that even in the most dystopian times, there are some cracks in those tough structures which light can seep through, creating something beautiful."

"That World Cup final was the nuttiest of *all* finals," said David.

"It was the final that marked the end of the ultimate discussion of who is the greatest football player of our time," said Edo.

"Look, may—" said David.

"May—?"

"May-be."

"Maybe? Come on. It was *meant* to be."

"Yeah, well, *maybe,*" said David, conceding a little.

"It was a match of pure Argentinian domination," said Edo dramatically. "Argentina broke the French spine for eighty minutes straight. I've *never* seen a world-champion France team look so helpless. Argentinians were attacking in packs like crazed wolves—defenders *and* attackers. Then, Mbappé defied all logic, scoring twice and levelling the match at 2-2 with ten minutes to go. Argentina needed to find superhuman strength not to drop their heads. Messi had to find both Ronaldinho and Cristiano within."

"Yeah, that was Messi's moment," said David gently. "He scored for Argentina in extra time!"

"But it was not solely about that goal," said Edo. "That was the one great moment he had to release his deepest magic and spread it to the rest of his squad. Anything else, France would have won it. Anything else and Kolo Muani's kick would have ended up in the net behind Emiliano Martínez in the last seconds of extra time with the result at 3-3. The French subs were already on the pitch celebrating the victory, but Martínez made the save of his life, spreading out like he had never spread before."

"What a *save* that was," said David, punching the air.

"Once it went to penalties, France never stood a chance," said Edo.

"Never!" said David. "Martínez did his job *right*. He got into the French players' heads and easily won it for Argentina. They couldn't pull the lever effectively—*not a chance*!"

"After the winning penalty by Montiel," said Edo. "The Argentinian players ran towards the scorer and Martínez. Still, Messi fell to his knees, and as he opened his arms, other players, one by one, turned around as if they were drawn into his tractor beam by pure magic, and they fell into a hug with the greatest human being that has ever played the game."

David bowed his head in recognition.

"Messi showed Mbappé," he said as they left the Wembley stadium.

"*Football won*," said Edo.

CHANGES

Manchester City Centre

June 2023

◇

Pep—Control Freak in Recovery

The Flexible System

Manchester was blue. Thousands of Manchester City fans filled the city centre to join the victory parade and salute their champions. It was a scorching summer day, nothing like the usual Manchester weather, but a few black clouds had gathered just as the bus with the players was supposed to show up.

Two days before, Manchester City had won the Champions League final for the first time in their history, completing the *treble*, having earlier won the FA Cup and Premier League.

People in blue shirts were climbing roofs, lamp posts, bus stops and trees to get into a good position to see the bus. The honk of trumpet horns played over the cheering fans.

"I can't believe you made me come here today, Edo," said David as they walked up Deansgate, the main road through the city centre.

"I didn't make you do anything," said Edo. "Don't put that on me. You wanted to see it for yourself, just as I did. Admit it. It's a special occasion. As you know, only once has a Premier

League club won the treble until now. We may not see this again in our lifetime."

"Yes, I am well aware," said David. "It was us in 1999, which makes it hurt more."

As David spoke, lightning struck a local roof, followed by a thunderous boom and heavy raindrops. It was the first rain Manchester had seen in over a month. The fans cheered loudly, basking in the sudden summer shower.

"Isn't this symbolic?" said David as they found a dry spot under a tree. "The first rain in over a month comes just as the Man City open bus is supposed to come this way."

"Yeah, but what's symbolic about it?" asked Edo. "I mean, look at these fans. They're as excited as they've ever been for this rain. It's the weather they're used to—the quenching rain of world domination. But for a Man United fan, the symbolism is *different,* obviously."

Cause we've got Guardiola, the fans sung loudly. *We've got Guardiola. Cause we've got Guardiola, so glad you're mine.*

"Guardiola's legacy at this point is unfortunately undeniable," David muttered.

"Yeah," said Edo. "After this season, no one can deny he's the greatest."

"Well," said David. "We can discuss that, my friend. As you said, he's not the *first* to win the treble. There's still the small question of Sir Alex Ferguson."

"Ferguson is a contender too, of course," said Edo.

"But yeah," said David. "Maybe we *all* need a certain Guardiola in our lives to keep persuading us we can achieve anything—someone who will look us in the eye and tell us there's nothing to be afraid of, that we've been through a lot worse *and* that we should lift our spirits."

"What he has done with City is beyond comparison," said Edo. "I don't remember a better team than this one, David. I really don't."

David nodded reluctantly.

"Sure," he said. "Apart from this Champions League trophy, he won five Premier League titles in the last six seasons. As painful as it is, Manchester has been blue for far too long, Edo."

"Unparalleled," said Edo.

"They say Pep Guardiola changed football," muttered David.

"He didn't just *change* football," said Edo. "He has been *changing* football for fifteen years! And he could only do that because he has been changing *himself* all along. From Barcelona to Munich, to Manchester. You can't change the world if you don't change yourself, David."

"His systems were always unmatched—at all those clubs," said David.

"Unmatched," agreed Edo. "And they've all been blessed with Guardiola's similar style of play. Yet, at the same time, they've all been very different systems."

"What do you mean?" said David as the rain poured harder and the fans sang even louder.

"What I mean is Barcelona was a strict system," said Edo. "Unique, yes! But also, strict. Only Messi was above the system. Pep controlled everyone else tightly. Bayern was different. Pep came to Munich wiser, more experienced, and more eager to experiment with life. And boy, did he experiment—in a way no one had ever witnessed. He experimented with player positions to the point of satire. Philipp Lahm could play in eight different positions under Pep. Same with Joshua Kimmich. The tough, inflexible Bayern system had become flexible, and Pep was flexible like never before. And by the same token, nowadays in Man City, there are elements of freedom which the old Pep from Barcelona couldn't even grasp."

"Interesting," said David.

"Actually," said Edo. "If anything finally got him to this Champions League trophy, it was his ability to change. He's a very different man from fifteen years ago when he got the job at Barcelona. The essence of his team is *very* different. When he renewed his contract with Man City at the end of 2022, Pep said that from day one, people had been changing, and the team had been changing, just as the opponents were changing, so he needed to change as well. He said, *We are not the same as we were at the beginning, but that is the secret*.[59]

"So how come he managed to win two Champions League titles with Barcelona?" said David. "Pep's Barcelona was very close to a perfect system. Some would say it was the strongest team that ever played the game. How did he create such a perfect system after only such a short time as manager—in his first managerial job? He certainly didn't have time to acquire all the valuable lessons that come with defeats and are necessary for creating the perfect system."

"Yeah," Edo said. "But even without it, I believe Pep learnt many lessons at Barcelona. First of all, he understood the philosophy of Barcelona even before he managed the first team, having spent most of his playing career in the club, right? Second, he was a tactical genius—even as a player. Pep was always obsessed with Johan Cruyff's idea of football, and he was privileged to be mentored by Cruyff, the football genius, as Pep called him.[60] So his understanding of Barcelona didn't begin in 2008 when he was appointed manager of Barcelona's first team, but in 1988, when he started playing for Barcelona C. Pep created a system based on a strong identity, with clear rules and patterns, but not so much freedom."

"Pep is a genius when it comes to other things as well," said David. "Communication, for instance. A great system can't work without great communication. Pep got that one right. Just like at Barcelona, *none* of those Manchester City successes would be possible without it."

"What kind of communication are you talking about?" said Edo, raising his voice above the rain and crowd.

"Communication between players, first of all, my friend," said David. "And at every single level of the organisation as well. Poor communication leads to inconsistency, and that's when a manager is at risk of losing control over the people above and below him. Communication is a proper skill which comes over time with practice, although some people have it naturally. But Pep, in particular, is an incredible communicator."

"Yeah," said Edo.

"Communication between players at Pep's Barcelona was so good that they barely needed words anymore," said David. "The game had evolved into mostly nonverbal communication, but the objective of where the ball needed to go was loud regardless. Busquets, Xavi and Iniesta could understand each other with a single wink so Tiki-taka football could flourish. But it wasn't just communication between players. The way Guardiola engages his players in the dressing room—his passion, tone, language, motion. The man *knows* how to send a message."

"Right," said Edo. "And with Pep's charisma on top of that, you get the real deal."

"The real deal," said David, pointing at Edo. "And Barcelona president Joan Laporta revealed on one occasion that Pep promised he would win everything if Barcelona appointed him. And bloody hell, he was right—*fourteen* trophies in four seasons!"

"Indeed," said Edo. "And Pep believed in his promise because he had the vision that comes when many pieces of wisdom come together. Pep has always followed his visions."

"His methods of persuasion were *unique* as well," said David. "Dani Alves said that if Pep had told him to jump off the third tier of Camp Nou, he would have done it because there must have been a good reason for it. And that was only Guardiola's *first* year in charge.

"And who *knows* what he told those boys before the 2011 final against Man United," said Edo. "If 2009 was an epic performance, how could you even describe what Barcelona did to United in 2011? That was arguably the most dominant final match performance ever."

David lowered his head.

"Yeah," he said. "Guardiola has put us through so much pain over the years."

"3-1 at Wembley," Edo said.

"I won't deny it," said David. "Barca murdered us that day. 3-1 doesn't do them justice. We had four attempts on goal in the whole game and guess how many they had."

"Twelve?" said Edo.

"*Bzzz* wrong, thanks for playing," said David, punching Edo on the shoulder. "Twenty-two, Edo. *Twenty-two* attempts against one of the strongest teams ever fielded—Ferguson's Man United. But that Barca team were unprecedented. I was shocked that Rooney even managed to score for us. I mean, it was a nice goal, but it was completely overshadowed by Pedro, Messi and Villa, who destroyed us—and all directed by Xavi and Iniesta, the legendary spine of Guardiola's idea of football. That match was simply a perfect representation of what Barcelona was in those days. They taught us a *proper* lesson. Actually, it was a proper *exception* to—"

"To the rule that hundreds of lessons are necessary to create a perfect system?" interrupted Edo.

David nodded.

"Exactly," he said. "However, after a while, Pep's talent wasn't enough anymore, and his lack of experience returned to haunt him. We saw it at the end of his Barcelona career when the system started to crumble. Pep lost his shit, and the players lost their patience with him."

"Ah, so that wasn't a perfect system either," said Edo.

"It couldn't be," said David, shaking his head. "Pep hadn't acquired enough losses as a coach to learn his lessons."

"True," said Edo. "And more importantly, there wasn't freedom in his team, which meant his system wasn't sustainable. Thierry Henry pretty much said that Pep became a control freak who tried to influence every aspect of the players' lives, both on and off the pitch. *Don't watch tennis, don't stay in the sun, don't go to Formula One, don't do this, don't do that, don't eat this, eat that—we are on a mission*, Henry said. So sure, Pep had techniques that brought Barcelona to glory, but in his last season in charge, the players were fed up with that."

"Why, because the system was too solid?" said David.

"It would seem that way," said Edo. "He knew what he was doing but seemed to lose the balance. I suppose his passion was too much, and he couldn't let players be—like a nagging parent."

"And he didn't have enough lessons in the bank to back it up," said David.

Edo nodded.

"The cracks appeared in 2012—Pep's last season at Barcelona," David said. "Dani Alves said, *That final year, if Pep told me to jump from the Camp Nou stands, I would have sprinted down the steps as fast as possible, but I wouldn't have jumped anymore*. That was the difference, I suppose. So yeah, Pep's magical system at Barca was unsustainable. He quickly set up a system that seemed perfect because he understood the club's philosophy and had the mind of a genius, but it couldn't be the perfect system."

"Players didn't buy into his *ideas* anymore," Edo said.

"That's the part of the system that was unsustainable," said David. "It was making the system imperfect. Persuasion is unsustainable. The perfect system has no persuasion, just motivation and communication. No one needs persuasion when they have already learnt *all* the lessons."

"You speak wisely," Edo said, bowing respectfully at his friend.

"His bakery destroyed *all* the bakeries in the street and ended up destroying itself," said David.

"Absolutely," said Edo. "Pep lost himself in his role. He lost the clarity. And he needed some time to recover from all the pressure he put on himself. After he left Barcelona, he spent a year in New York contemplating."

"Right," said David.

"Even baking too many Shepherd's loaves can end badly," said Edo.

"True," said David. "And Pep even admitted on one occasion that he doesn't have all the answers. He said, *Often, when I don't know something, I act in front of the players as if I do. I do it so they believe I have the answers, giving them the confidence to play.*"[61]

"I am sure there was no bluffing with Messi, though," said Edo. "Communication is about sending a message, but to truly connect with someone requires presence and attention. And Messi felt Guardiola's vision."

"Yeah, Messi didn't need much explanation," said David.

"Correct, David," said Edo. "And I think you just got the answer to how Guardiola managed to create such a perfect system at Barcelona in such a short period—Messi!"

Haaland and Grealish

Brothers in Awareness

"Still nothing, Edo?"

Edo gazed up the street, squinting in the rain for any sign of the Man City team bus.

"Still nothing," he said as the distant thunder rolled. Edo took out his flask of tea, poured a cup and offered it to David, who shook his head.

"Ever since Messi, Guardiola had been trying to find a formula to win the Champions League," said Edo. "For twelve long years, he tried. But he couldn't. He simply couldn't."

"Something wasn't right," said David.

"No," said Edo, filling his cup and putting the tea away. "But then, a couple of years ago, his perspective changed deeply."

"How do you know that?" said David,

"Have you heard of Erling Haaland and Jack Grealish?" Edo said, looking out for the bus again.

David grinned.

"They were the pair who proved Pep was ready for the big leagues and that Pep sought balance," said Edo. "Because, as we already established, Pep is a bit of a control freak. And at Barcelona, that's what ultimately cost him his position. In an attempt to establish absolute control, he ended up in several fights with players who were probably uncontrollable. The uncontrollable ones were usually authentic players who brought something extra to the club, but also, they were players whose unique perspective on the world made them difficult to fit into Pep's system. And look, we all know Pep rates the *system* above everything. It's the system that has brought him glory. He couldn't deal with Ronaldinho, Ibrahimović, or Yaya Touré."

"True," said David.

"Ibrahimović couldn't stand it," said Edo. "So he called Guardiola a spineless coward."

David laughed.

"They *certainly* didn't like each other," he said.

"The only one who was ever beyond Pep's system—who was allowed to express himself fully was Messi," said Edo. "Messi could get the ball in his own box or his opponent's. He could even lift the ball off the ground, which was considered a mortal sin in Pep's Barcelona. He didn't need to run in defence unless he felt like it. But every other player who tried to be bigger than the system was quickly dismissed."

David nodded solemnly.

"Wow," he said. "And that brings us to twelve years without the Champions League trophy."

"Correct," said Edo. "But it seems that Pep finally figured out that without such uniqueness in his team, it would be hard to win the Champions League. So he *has* changed. He faced his biggest fear of *losing control* and signed Jack Grealish—the one who has his ways—*The last English maverick*, as the English media called him. It's easy to see that Grealish has an aura around his head."

"What do you mean, Edo?" said David.

"Well, you know," said Edo. "You can hear it in the way he speaks and deals with people with *humility*."

"Are you sure about that?" said David. "I remember him joking at Miguel Almirón's expense, suggesting he was a shitty player.[62] For me, that was a sign of disrespect rather than humility. And is the damn bus here yet, Edo?"

Edo checked again and shook his head.

"Well," he said. "It's only disrespectful to those who think too highly of themselves—those in the grip of ego. Otherwise, it's just a joke. And Grealish often jokes at his own expense. He can take a joke—and he can take criticism. He's a showman!"

"Yeah, a showman with an alcohol problem," said David. "I'm sure he is going to get pissed again today."

"Sure," said Edo. "Grealish has his flaws, but he is honest and sincere. And that requires a *lot* of clarity. Pep wanted him at City so badly. He wanted that aura in his team. He couldn't resist Jack's realness. You see, even though he is such a good player—capable of scoring remarkable goals—Jack admitted he could be stubborn and selfish when he was at Aston Villa. He said he should have been more of a team player in various situations, regardless of the mad skills he possessed.[63] Grealish is a man who speaks and plays from the heart. And as such, he's been a great test for Guardiola."

"Is that why his adaptation process at Manchester City has been everything but simple?" said David. "They'd been waiting for him for almost two years to get up to their level."

"It's likely because of that, yeah," said Edo. "Grealish reckoned he was much freer at Villa than at City, where everything is more structured. He said it was obviously going to change his game a little bit. *I am never going to be the same player that I was because now I play for a different club, a different team and a different manager.*[64] Back at Villa, Jack had all the space to be who he was—to expose his true self with which he was so well connected. His creativity on the pitch was outstanding, and he played from so deep in his heart."

The crowd began to get restless again, whistling for a bit before breaking out in song once more.

"And then Man City came knocking on Jack's door," Edo said. "And in Pep's perfect system, Grealish struggled to balance his true self and the system's requirements."

"Spot on," said David.

"However!" said Edo, holding up his finger as usual. "Even though Jack didn't make a significant contribution in his first season, he didn't fall out with Guardiola either, which proved that Pep's *personal* work was paying off—that he was loosening his control and putting his faith in mavericks. Pep said Grealish needs to be who he is, and that's all he expects from him—*To go out there and try to do the best for himself and all of them.*"[65]

"That was a big step for Guardiola, wasn't it?" said David.

"It was a huge step," said Edo. "Pep recently said, *Life is about controlling what you can and letting the uncontrollable be—it is what it is.*[66] I believe his experience with Grealish was enough for Pep to expose himself to the biggest challenge."

The thunder growled powerfully, and Edo punched the air.

"Erling Haaland!" he yelled in David's face.

"What?" said David.

"Could there have been any bigger challenge for Guardiola than the man whose childhood hero was Zlatan Ibrahimović?"[67]

"Well done to Guardiola then, right?" said David, applauding gently as a raindrop hit his nose.

"Massive well done to Guardiola," said Edo. "Haaland is *untameable*. With his unpredictable runs, Haaland *breaks* tactical structures and defensive systems. But that's not all he breaks. You know, his untameable character isn't limited to the pitch. Oh, *no*!"

"Interesting," said David. "So how come Pep managed to work with Haaland but couldn't work it out with Ibrahimović?"

Edo thought for a moment.

"Well," he said. "Both sides needed a lot of awareness to make it work. When Haaland joined City, he said his dream was to score five goals from five touches.[68] Guardiola's reaction was to say he would be happier if Haaland got more involved in the game and touched the ball more.[69] So you see, David, Haaland had to give up on some of his dreams and lose some of his freedom to serve the system. And Pep needed to relinquish some control over that system."

"I see," said David.

"Yep," said Edo. "And back in the day, Pep and Ibrahimović were both too rigid in their own ways. Pep has changed a lot since, and Haaland is also much softer than Ibra was. Pep said that football players need to have high ego but not too high. And he was referring to Haaland when he just got to City. But honestly, David, it's just about being aware."

"Aware?" said David.

"Yes, David—aware of your ego—aware of the role you play—aware of the thoughts and emotions that the role consists of."

"Aware of the role you play," David muttered.

"On the other hand," said Edo. "Lack of awareness of the role creates suffering."

"The same as when I suffer when Man United lose?" said David.

"Yeah, pretty much the same," said Edo. "And just as Cristiano suffers when he loses—when he isn't up to his own standards—when he is on the bench or when he misses a penalty."

"So what's the difference for those who are aware?" said David, standing up and moving closer to Edo to get above the noise of the trumpet.

Edo paused momentarily, looking into the sky to formulate an answer.

"With awareness comes the wisdom that all those structures you identify with are just part of the role you have created," he said. "That role is not essentially who you are. It's not a permanent role either, David. And someone who can let it go, stepping out of conditioned structures, can become limitless. That's when life becomes a journey full of challenges. Haaland still grows through wins and defeats, but there's no identification with winning or losing—at least not to the same extent. He goes through life, experiencing it fully but not identifying with objects too much—sometimes pushing harder, sometimes hanging back. Stepping out of those concepts doesn't mean losing them, though. It means you become *aware* of them. Erling Haaland is still the Erling Haaland who plays for Manchester City and has Manchester United as his rival. He's still a football player and an incredible striker—a Norwegian. Once a person is aware, identifying with those concepts can't be complete. Haaland isn't a soldier of the system, David. He's free even in the most captive establishments. When you are free in that way, you change your whole perspective on suffering. You recognise the lessons inherent in defeat and even the beauty in trauma. And there can even be gratitude for those things. There's still suffering, but it's conscious suffering. It doesn't stop you. It moves you."

David put his hand on Edo's shoulder.

"Too right, my friend," he said.

"Of course, sometimes ego takes over," said Edo. "Especially when the stakes are high. But you'll be alright if you're in touch with your essence. Haaland is a serial winner, but when he loses, he recovers quickly and keeps going. He forgets about the defeat and stays present. As Pep said, *When Haaland doesn't score, he's frustrated, but only for five minutes. After that, his mindset returns to the right position, and he does the job he must do.*"[70]

"What a player!" David said, shaking his head, looking up and noticing the rain was getting lighter.

"Meditation!" blurted Edo. "That's what puts Haaland in such a helpful state of mind."

"That's right," said David. "Haaland is big on meditation."

"Meditation helps build focus as well," said Edo. "Because only when you are aware of your thoughts can you put attention on one, rather than compulsively reacting to all of them. Haaland doesn't focus on, *I missed a clear chance*, but rather on *I will score the next one*."

"So meditation is the way forward," David muttered.

"It's like making a full load of Shepherd's loaves," said Edo. "Only you don't get distracted when your oven breaks or customers go to Arafat's. It's when you learn and love the whole process with all life's challenges. Ultimately, you're good to yourself because you are fulfilled by what you do regardless of how many loaves of bread you sell. Winning and losing is just part of that process. You burn the bread but deliver the next one, regardless."

David nodded.

"Being aware of your ego keeps you calm inside but still ruthless in front of the goal," he said, smiling.

A Team With No Superstars

When Truth Is Not Sought Externally

Things were firing up, and the music got louder as the bus finally approached. The fans exploded with euphoria as Erling Haaland appeared in the first row holding the Champions League trophy. Pep Guardiola looked fulfilled on the next bus, smoking a cigar and saluting the fans alongside his management team.

"Look at the players," David said. "Off the chains, they do seem free. Guardiola is not even on the same bus with them. The change has truly taken place."

Haaland and Jack Grealish were raving shirtless in the heavy rain and running the show while the rest of the players danced to the DJ's rhythm and swigged on bottles of champagne.

"Erling Haaland *is* a new football superstar," said David as the buses passed through. "And he's a Manchester City superstar as well."

"Yes," said Edo. "But you see, that's exactly what Pep is trying to avoid. He doesn't want superstars in his team."

"We can't run from the fact that Haaland's influence is huge," said David. "He'll stay remembered as a bigger player than, for instance—Julián Álvarez."

Edo laughed.

"Well, that's a collective, society-made truth," he said.

A group of fans flew past them, chasing the buses.

"What do you mean by society-made truth?" said David, watching them fly by.

"Well, look," said Edo. "The truth that tells us the better man is the one who has more money, is admired more, and has a bigger base of followers. Or that a better man is the one who has more goals to his name."

"Well, yeah," said David.

"Well, no," said Edo. "That's the most average way to see the world, David. As of June 12, 2023, there are 8,037,112,600 people worldwide, meaning there are that same number of unique truths. Therefore, it's unfair to say one person's truth is worth more than another's just because a society-made truth tells us to think that. Society says you're successful according to certain values or you're a failure. And that couldn't be further from the truth."

"From *your* truth?" said David.

"Yes, from my truth!" said Edo, firing up. "And *my* truth says we are all worth the same, no matter what we do or what our roles are. I refuse to let society tell me when I'm being a good or a bad boy. And I believe that's the only way we can find our personal truths—that we're already complete and perfect, just as we are, and that we fit perfectly in this inexplicable system called the universe. And that's when we can truly create, by the way."

"So that's your subjective perception of the world?" David said. "That's your truth, my friend?"

"Yes, David," said Edo. "That *is* my truth, but the moment you connect to the idea that you are perfect as you are, you connect with your personal truth, and you don't need other truths. That truth is beyond all the truths based on mind-made subjective perceptions. That truth is neither right nor wrong. It simply is. It's the universal truth that we all carry."

"You can't tell me Álvarez is worth the same as Haaland in that team," said David. "You can't say that Kyle Walker is worth the same as Kevin De Bruyne at Man City."

"That's *exactly* what I'm trying to tell you, David," said Edo. "Kyle Walker *is* worth the same as Kevin De Bruyne in that team. Yes, the number of goals or assists shows how De Bruyne is worth more than Walker. But those are the societal concepts that take you further from the truth. The fundamental truth is that every single player of Manchester City is of equal worth. And that's why they are the strongest team in the world."

"What?" said David. "De Bruyne is not replaceable in *any* system!"

"Are you sure about that?" said Edo. "The other day, De Bruyne got injured in the first half of the final against Inter and City managed to win the game, regardless."

As the parade pulled off into the distance, the pair stood watching the fans run after the the buses.

"And what a game it was," said Edo. "It was a game of the finest of margins. And it could have gone both ways, but Rodri's goal was enough for City to claim their first Champions League. Pep was finally relieved. It was a *proper* final."

"Exactly," said David. "It was a true final in Istanbul—a tough game against a very defensive Italian team in strange circumstances in front of a peculiar audience. And City deserved to win it. Yeah, they were the best team this season *by far*, but since it was a final, City weren't in their usual shape, and you can't judge De Bruyne's contribution based on the final in a neutral stadium. Finals are *always* strange."

"In that case," said Edo. "Remember the 2018/19 season when De Bruyne got injured for over half a season?"

David nodded.

"They won the league that season as well, right?" he muttered.

"Exactly," said Edo. "City won it with ninety-eight points, while unbelievable Liverpool finished with ninety-seven. Even that mighty Liverpool side couldn't take them down. And what do you think Kevin De Bruyne's season contribution was? I'll tell you. It was two goals and two assists."

"Yeah, I remember that," said David. "Bernardo Silva took his place and did it well. Which is good because between Liverpool and Man City, I always chose City."

"Fair enough," said Edo. "But again, it wasn't Bernardo Silva who won the title. The *system* won the title. Anyone was replaceable once the system worked—when everybody knew their role—even if that role changed from game to game. And Man City are who they are at the moment because *all* the players accept their roles, and they know the team needs every role to work for Pep's system to balance."

"Okay, okay," said David. "I agree that accepting and understanding your role is important, but what counts is how you can exploit that role to contribute to the system. I remember the game between City and Liverpool at the beginning of 2019. Liverpool started the game seven points clear of City at the top of the table. They would have had a ten-point advantage if they'd won, and the race would be pretty much over. But City put in an unbelievable performance and claimed a 2-1 victory."

"Exactly!" said Edo. "Without De Bruyne, the system won."

"Okay," said David. "I admit, rather painfully, that it was amazing. Agüero scored the first from the narrowest angle before Firmino equalised in the second half. Then, Leroy Sané made it 2-1. It was an outstanding performance by City, and instead of Liverpool going ten points clear, they reduced the gap to just four points. It was a game that shuffled the cards in the title race and contributed to City's eventual title. And the funniest bit is stories were floating around that Guardiola would lose his job as City manager if he'd lost the match."

"That's crazy!" said Edo.

"In this crazy world, it's unbelievable that Guardiola has never been sacked," said David.

"Exactly," said Edo. "Neither has his biggest rival, Jürgen Klopp, who, by the way, also confirmed that the system is *the* most important thing. He said, *The beautiful thing about football is that you can't do anything alone.*"

"What?" said David. "Why do you always have to bring him into it? Isn't it enough that I am attending the City victory parade. Seriously, show some respect."

Edo shrugged.

"Sorry, but it's true," he said.

"Sure it is," said David. "It *is* all about the team. Only the collective synergy of many individuals can bring progress to the system. A perfect system can arise only when people of different skills come together."

"Exactly," said Edo.

"It's like having a bakery where the dough-maker is worth the same as the CEO of the bakery," said David. "There's no jealousy, but everybody does what they do best. Support within the team—among employees—would flourish, and people would go to work happy, knowing it means something much bigger than personal validation."

"That's right," said Edo. "And to make that happen, you need a group of people comfortable with who they are and what their roles are. Call it whatever you like, but it's about connecting to your true self—your inner role. Because only in that state of consciousness can you maximise the potential in your outer role—whatever that entails at any given time—and still be equal to the next man. You remember—builders, warriors, philosophers, artists, servants? That's why Manchester City is the best team in the world—no egos in the squad, David."

"True," said David. "They have no egos, and there is empathy for each other, but they are still ruthless toward other teams, having no compassion for them whatsoever."

"They are balancing their inner and outer roles," said Edo. "To master life—"

"—is to find a balance between Ronaldo and Ronaldinho," interjected David.

"Yeah!" said Edo, looking at his friend and then up at the sky. "After winning the title in his first season at the club, and even though he wasn't on the level of the rest of the team, Grealish said that the *togetherness* in the dressing room struck him from day one. And when they won the Premier League title this year, İlkay Gündoğan said that this season, the atmosphere at the training ground and in the team felt even more special.[71] That's what Haaland and Grealish brought to the team."

"Awareness?" said David.

"They don't care if society, or in this case, their audience, praises De Bruyne because he's the one who prevails in all the major statistical records," said Edo. "That's why Pep's relationship with the media isn't the best. He doesn't allow anybody to create superstars out of his players. He protects their personal truths, and thus he also protects the system."

"So why did it take so long for Grealish to find himself a role in that team?" said David.

Edo took a deep breath.

"As we already established, at Villa, Grealish was free to expose his personal truth to the fullest," he said. "And at Man City, everyone has a role, and acting outside that structure isn't possible, even when going beyond means expressing your absolute potential rather than egoic needs. Pep wants to use Grealish's potential and synchronise it with his own potential and, therefore, the team's potential. But the process was challenging for someone as real as Jack. Let's see if he can consciously play his role within the system and maintain his personal truth. Will Grealish be able to balance his personal truth with the system's requirements? Can he use his role as a tool to align with the potential of Pep Guardiola and Manchester City?"

"So awareness *is* the key?" said David.

"Awareness is the key!" said Edo. "If Jack loses his awareness, his personal truth will disappear, and he will become just another soldier of the system—chained. He might even seek his salvation through excessive drinking."

"So Jack Grealish, as the last maverick, is gone either way?" said David.

Edo looked up at the grey clouds beginning to clear.

"Only Messi could have been the maverick in Pep's system," he said.

Learning From Each Other

One Point Each

Some of the noisy crowd followed the team's bus while the rest headed towards the main stage at St Peter's Square.

David and Edo strolled along John Dalton Street as the rain stopped and started continuously.

"Pep's journey has been an exceptional one," said David. "And although he has made us the second-best team in Manchester, I must admit he's done some astonishing things."

"Very true, David," said Edo. "Pep learns from everybody and everything. That's why his journey has been so great. He learnt from Barcelona, Munich and Manchester."

"Yeah, he gets the best out of his defeats," said David. "Pep once said that a hard crash can serve as the impetus you need because it unites the group. *You're at your lowest point, but it's also what could save you if you are able, as a group, to pull together and convert the despair into positive energy.*"[72]

"Well, that's what happened against Real Madrid in 2021," said Edo. "It was, perhaps, the most painful defeat of Pep's career. During the game, Man City had everything and lost it all within a minute. But after the game, Pep appeared calm in front of the cameras. He said, *Football is unpredictable, and sometimes you need to accept it.*[73] By accepting the situation as it is, we unlock the full potential of a situation and look for resolution more naturally. By accepting, we can make the most of the situation, good or bad, and understand it as a part of the process. That's why he wasn't desperate after that game. He was ready to get back to lifting his players right away."

David shook his head in admiration.

"Then, this year, he came back bigger and destroyed Real Madrid 4-0," he said. "What a game that was—a superb presentation of what he had learnt from that painful master—defeat."

"Yes," said Edo. "Defeats, victories, and draws. Pep learns from everything—even draws."

"Draws?" said David, scratching his head. "What is there to learn from draws? Didn't we already have this conversation, Edo? There is no progress in a draw."

"On the contrary," said Edo, holding up a finger. "For the man who takes life as his teacher, progress is everywhere. A draw can be a beautiful thing!"

"Oh, come on," said David. "No draw has ever been beautiful!"

"Not true!" said Edo.

The rain intensified again, and Edo and David sheltered under a roof as they approached St Peter's Square, where a man was playing a saxophone accompanied by a group of City fans—*Rodri's on fire. Your defence is terrified.*

"Fine," said David. "I challenge you to give me one good game that ended in a draw!"

Edo thought for a moment. "We don't need to go far in history to find one, David," he said. "How about that Manchester City–Liverpool match in 2022? I believe that game had everything a beautiful draw can offer."

"Oh, come on," said David. "Two of the worst clubs in the world drawing? Seriously, Edo, you're testing my patience now."

"Hear me out," said Edo. "Liverpool had somehow closed a fourteen-point gap with City and were now only a single point behind when they finally met at the Etihad, with just eight games remaining in the season. And even after two crazy years that changed everything we knew about everything, those two clubs still dominated the game. And this game had the potential to decide the championship. It was a true clash of the titans—Guardiola versus Klopp—De Bruyne versus Salah. And it ended in a spectacular draw."

"Sounds like an anti-climax," said David.

"It wasn't," said Edo. "Kevin De Bruyne shocked Liverpool with a goal just five minutes in. He was utterly immense and carried his whole team. He was just too strong for them—for the rest of the league. To his opponents, KDB was on a different level. Anyway, only a few minutes later, Diogo Jota equalised. But City dominated the game, and Jesus scored to give City the lead before half-time. And things didn't look good for Liverpool. But somehow, Klopp's team demonstrated their mental strength, and Mané banged in an equaliser a few minutes into the second half.

David rolled his eyes.

"Great story, Edo," he said. "But it still sounds like a boring draw to me."

"You're just saying that because it's City and Liverpool," said Edo. "But listen, the match ended 2–2—exquisite balance, my dear friend."

"Fine," said David. "It *was* an amazing game with chances all over the pitch—a beautiful story with incredible protagonists and goals. But in the end, it was still a depressing draw and hence pointless. All that for nothing—"

"Pointless?" barked Edo. "Nothing is pointless, David. Quite the opposite. The final whistle of the match displayed the full potential a draw can carry."

"Oh yeah?"

"Yep. Guardiola and Klopp engaged in the lord of all high fives. Afterwards, they hugged each other, releasing the peaceful outcome's dormant power. The energy was bursting out of that high five—the energy of *balance*."

"It was impotent energy," said David, still unconvinced. "Nothing more than stagnant energy lacking any evolutionary potential."

"You can't say you didn't see the evolutionary potential in that high five," said Edo. "Seriously, man. It oozed gratitude, stillness, and inspiration. It's a different kind of evolution."

"It brought nothing to anybody," growled David.

Edo shook his head in frustration.

"Not true!" he said. "It brought incredible clarity and acceptance into Pep's interview after the match. He said that he wanted to win the league, but it didn't matter as long as they performed admirably as they did against such a strong Liverpool side. *We were so good, and all our fans enjoyed it so much.*[74] What a moment."

David screwed up his nose.

"So Pep meant that he didn't care if he won the league as long as his team had given it all?"

"Pretty much," said Edo. "You see, Pep isn't solely interested in winning. He's more interested in creating something greater than himself—great leagues, great teams, great fan bases, great national teams, great football."

"Great national teams?" said David. "Have you lost your mind? Pep has never managed a national team."

"I know that David," said Edo. "But look, Spain won the World Cup when Pep coached Barcelona. Germany won it when Pep coached Bayern. Even England have improved since Pep arrived in Manchester."

David sighed and shook his head again.

"It's no coincidence," said Edo. "Pep's players were at the core of all those national teams. His philosophy was at the core of them."

"I must admit, it's an interesting idea," said David, looking skyward as the rain slowed.

The pair strolled across the tram station towards the main stage where thousands of humans in drenched sky-blue shirts filled St Peter's Square. All generations of Manchester City fans had turned up for the historic moment.

"It might actually make sense," David muttered, having thought about it some more.

"Yes, Pep has learnt from everything," said Edo. "But what makes him even greater is that he teaches others equally without keeping his knowledge to himself. Man! Arteta was close to winning the Premier League with Arsenal. Vincent Kompany won the Championship with Burnley. Xavi Hernandez won La Liga with Barcelona. Xabi Alonso is cooking something spicy at Leverkusen as well. All of them were Pep's students."

"You're right," said David. "That's truly admirable."

"The whole Premier League has changed its way of playing," said Edo. "All the teams are playing out from the back these days. People said Pep wouldn't be able to play his type of football in England. Now the whole of England plays his football."

David shook his head and punched Edo in the shoulder.

"Wow," he shouted over the noisy crowd. "Okay, I'm starting to get what you're saying, my friend."

"Pep's influence is beyond comparison," shouted Edo. "He's both master and student of his opponents. He *always* supports other managers and urges owners to give managers time before sacking them. Pep admires the Brighton manager Roberto De Zerbi. And even though he is many levels above him, Guardiola said he learns from De Zerbi."[75]

"True," said David.

"You should listen to the interview of Guardiola after that great draw against Liverpool," said Edo. "Pep said, *I don't know if Jürgen respects me, but he has to know that I respect him a lot. He has made me a better manager. His teams are always positive and aggressive. They want to score goals, and they attack. And I try to imitate him in that sense.*"

"I see," said David.

"Right?" said Edo. "And you see, I'm not sure if victory or defeat would create the right environment for such words to be allowed. In victory such words would be unnecessary, and in defeat, such words would be inappropriate. Yet, after a draw—a peaceful outcome—different perspectives arise. The field of *clarity* arises."

"The field of clarity?" said David.

"Yes, pal," said Edo. "The flow of knowledge was wide open for the benefit of both managers. Pep learnt from Klopp, and Klopp learnt from Pep."

"So a draw then?" said David, smiling and putting his arm on Edo's shoulder.

"One point each, my dear friend," said Edo. "One point each!"

Pep Guardiola wandered deliriously onto the main stage, wearing a fresh dry shirt.

Edo and David watched the show on the big screen from a distance.

This is the best parade in the rain, Guardiola said. *If there were no rain, it wouldn't be Manchester. We don't want sunshine.*[76]

The crowd applauded him passionately.

"You see that," said Edo. "Even though Pep Guardiola was heavily identified with warm-weather Barcelona, he wasn't afraid to challenge that identity or change his systems and personal values on the way."

"People don't like to see their heroes change, though," said David. "That's the thing about change."

"They don't, that's true," Edo agreed. "That's because people tend to identify with their heroes and the specific values those heroes bring to the table. Unless they've learnt about the importance of change from Pep himself, Man City fans won't like it once Pep moves on."

"It's actually about *them* rather than their heroes, isn't it?" said David.

"Look," said Edo. "If you fall under the pressure of your followers and resist the change, those values that once got you to the top will eventually bring you down. Mourinho is a great example of that."

"Oh, here we go again," David barked. "If you insist on bringing Mourinho into this, Edo, please remember that he just brought Roma to a European final for the second year in a row."

"Well, sure, that *sounds* great," said Edo. "But is it really great? His football hasn't changed since he won the Champions League with Inter in 2010. It's the same style of football his teams have been playing all along."

"Well, that style brings him trophies!" said David, punching Edo once again.

"Yes," said Edo, rubbing his shoulder. "But José was once on top of the world. His football made history back in the day. And I'm sorry, but we can't pretend winning the Conference League is the same as winning the Champions League. His style is still a winning style but on a way lower scale."

"It is still the winning style, okay?" said David.

"I don't know, David. Just compare Mourinho's team with Guardiola's team—Mou's football and Pep's football. It's like a different sport."

"Mou didn't disappoint his supporters, though," said David. "He never changed, and that's why he still has an army of passionate fans."

"Yeah, passionate fans who also don't change," said Edo.

Several City players came onto the main stage, holding up the three trophies comprising the treble. The crowd burst into a euphoric roar, jumping up and down.

"I'll tell you a secret," Edo shouted.

"Go on then," said David.

Edo leaned into his friend and looked him in the eyes as if he was about to reveal something significant.

"At the end of the day," Edo said. "*Everyone* changes. It's just that some resist change as hard as possible, while others accept change easier."

"I suppose," said David.

"After Roma's Europa League final against Sevilla two weeks ago, José pulled out his old favourite excuse and blamed the referee for his loss," said Edo.[77] "But I admit that in the build-up to the game, I *did* see changes in Mourinho. After his Roma side qualified for the final of the Europa League, he didn't appear in front of the media as *The Special One*, but as a man who said that he believed he was a good coach yet was humble enough to say that he owed Roma's place in the final to his players."

"You see," said David.

"*Everything* changes in its essence," said Edo. "And *nothing* will ever be the same."

"Everything?" said David." Like what?"

"Like *everything*" Edo insisted. "Cristiano plays in Saudi Arabia now. Messi did two years in prison at dystopian PSG, despite having spent his career at Barcelona—the club that was *Més Que Un Club*, which was all about investing in the youth academy and nurturing the team spirit. Somehow, Lionel ended up part of a team showered in gold that is more famous for its friction between players than anything else. And now he's moving to Inter Miami in America."

"Okay," said David.

Edo took a deep breath.

"It's like this," he said. "Messi said that on a personal level, he hadn't been happy during his last two years at PSG and wanted to go back to Barcelona, but he didn't want any more of the drama he experienced when he left Barcelona. Hence, Inter Miami."[78]

"It's crazy that the Paris fans booed Messi at his farewell game for PSG," said David.

"Exactly," said Edo. "And at the same time, Ibrahimović received a Totti-esque farewell from the Milan fans. A lot of tears were spilt all around San Siro. Despite changing clubs nine times in his career, it looks like Ibra was crowned a prince of Milan after all."

"Yeah, he got under their skin eventually," said David. "It was an emotional farewell—not *quite* like Totti's—but yeah."

"Everything changes in its essence," said Edo. "The World Cup is suddenly played in December rather than mid-year. Chelsea's owner is no longer a Russian but an American. Arsenal have started playing well. Leicester were relegated. Pep is bringing free spirits into his team."

"Arafat is selling more bread than I am, and not long ago it seemed his bakery was going out of business," said David. "The pandemic has crippled the world. Wars are raging."

"The Super League is knocking on the door!" said Edo.

"Yes!" said David. "It seems that the world is going mad, my friend."

"It seems like that," said Edo. "Many people argue that these changes are bad, that we are changing for the worst and should return to the old normal. But I disagree with that. We're not supposed to go back to the old life, David. It's all about evolution. It's about moving forward and learning, remember?"

"Yeah, I remember," said David. "We're meant to see our mistakes as lessons—individually *and* collectively. The world changes all the time, and that's fine. I suppose it's good to change. Every change is a step forward on the path of evolution. But the Super League, Edo? How can we be all right with that change? How?"

"Yes!" said Edo, impressed with his friend's words. "But if we, somehow, *could* operate against the laws of the universe and manage to go back to what was before, that would only mean at one point we would end up where we are now."

"Like spinning in a circle," muttered David.

"Exactly," said Edo. "*Just* like spinning in a circle. It might not be obvious, but we needed *all* those those shitty situations to keep evolving—pandemics, wars, Paris Saint-Germain, the Super League. There are *always* good things in bad situations."

David nodded.

"Everything changes," said Edo. "*Except* Ronaldinho consciousness, which is absolute, and where good equals bad. Ronaldinho still plays beach football with the same smile just like he always has."

David laughed and shook his head as the Man City players danced on the stage.

"It might seem like we're devolving and in a bad place, but sometimes years pass, and we realise it wasn't all that bad," said David. "Which doesn't mean I won't fight against the Super League again."

"And this is all part of the collective consciousness rising as well," said Edo. "Sometimes we need to suffer so our old thinking patterns dissolve, allowing liberating new patterns to emerge."

"Great stuff, my friend," said David.

"To become free like Ronaldinho," whispered Edo, raising a hand dramatically.

David nodded.

"Maybe the dawn of the Super League will mark a great shift in consciousness," Edo said.

"Which, by the way, *still* doesn't mean I won't fight against it when it comes!"

"Yes, you have made that perfectly clear," said Edo. "As I said, reverting to the way things were is only possible in fiction because perpetual growth is the nature of the universe. To experience the Renaissance, humans *had* to go through the Middle Ages. Nobody went back to ancient Rome, for God's sake. We kept evolving. And if the Renaissance happened after a thousand years of the Middle Ages, then we can expect to have at least one decent period once all this turmoil is over—if we're still here, that is."

"And with all these lessons, we would surely *blossom*," said David, raising his fists in the usual way. "Surely, it's just a question of how deep into the cesspit we can sink before we start to resurface—and how profound our lesson will be, my friend."

"That's wise, David," said Edo with a grin.

"Sometimes, though," said David. "It's hard for us proper fans to align with change. The pandemic was challenging for us, with only limited stadium seats. Also, they only allowed fans with a premium membership to participate in the ticket ballot at one point—as if it wasn't enough that ticket prices were a hundred quid. Football has become a game for the elites, Edo. God knows what prices they would charge if the Super League went forward. What would football look like? What would the clubs become?"

Edo put his hand on David's shoulder.

"It's about my Man United identity," said David. "I see that now, Edo. I'm protecting my Man United identity. But it's still *my* identity. And it would be endangered by the Super League."

"At least you know now what's behind your fear," said Edo.

David looked stunned, as if he suddenly realised thousands of sky-blue shirts surrounded him.

"Have you ever heard about the Hillsborough tragedy?" Edo asked.

"Of course, Edo," said David, hanging his head. "I'm not from the Middle Ages."

Edo nodded.

"Almost a hundred Liverpool fans died that day," he said. "Liverpool versus Forest—the 1989 FA Cup semi-final in Sheffield. Apparently, instead of funnelling fans towards the two less-crowded pens, police gave the green light to let them pour into the Leppings Lane End—an already overcrowded central area behind the goal. And horribly, there was a high fence preventing fans from escaping to the safety of the pitch. Many of the fans died from compressive asphyxia whilst standing."

David kept looking at the ground and shook his head.

"But you see," Edo continued. "After that, things didn't revert to the old way. An evolution took place, and everything changed for fans—the era of the *new normal* began. Before Hillsborough, over thirty thousand fans used to stand in single terraces behind the goal at Manchester United's Stretford End, the Holte End at Villa Park or in the Kop End at Anfield. Plastic seats replaced those vast steps of concrete standing room, and they demolished many famous old stadiums. They forced clubs to follow safety-first laws to prevent similar disasters in future. To this day, you can't drink alcohol in the stands at a Premier League match."

"So annoying! We are way too controlled these days," said David. "Real fans didn't support those changes. They wanted to go back to the old ways."

"Same old story isn't it, David?" said Edo. "But change happened regardless. The profile of fans changed after Hillsborough. Ticket prices went up. Aggressive individuals were no longer welcome, while women and children started filling the void. Football matches became a family event. Eventually, football became a truly supportive environment. Football today fights for equality like no other sport or thing."

"Oh yeah?" said David.

"You see," said Edo. "In every *seemingly* bad situation, there's a space for healing. More often than not, though, people start seeking meaning in those movements which support equality and in doing so, they make it about themselves again. Just as you identify with Manchester United to feel part of something bigger and to be part of the club's success, they now identify with movements, and the idea of *support* becomes a tool for people to flaunt their egos. Those movements become part of their identity—*I am a supporter of equality*.

"Makes sense," said David.

"True support can't be achieved with ego," said Edo.

"Well, yes," said David. "But I believe identifying with such equality movements is a step forward on our journey, nonetheless."

"Probably," said Edo. "But as soon as there is identification, there will be enemies—for instance, people who don't support those movements. Subsequently, there will be people who *identify* as non-supporters of those movements, and just like that, we have another environment of winning and losing, and suffering—battles between egos."

Edo took a deep breath, noticing a tiny streak of crisp blue among the grey clouds.

"One day, my dear friend, there won't be any identification," he said gently.

The Day Ronaldo Became a Child Again

Humbled by Love

"Even the most rigid structures will eventually dissolve, and we will become free," Edo said as they watched the official party die down and the people leaving the city centre. "Even the CR7 structure will one day turn to dust."

"Are you sure about that?" said David. "The idea of CR7 has become so huge. It's everywhere. Before Ronaldo stops identifying with that structure, other people will need to stop identifying with it first. Ronaldo's followers keep him alive. And there are more and more of them every day. He's now spreading his name to other continents, becoming big in Saudi Arabia—showing them what a god-like man looks like."

"Makes sense," said Edo. "But he still might break free despite his environment. After all, we are all responsible for our own lives. The more conscious we get, the more we take back control and the less we act according to other's expectations. We saw the trouble caused by Cristiano's inability to live up to his god-like image during his last spell at United. But how conscious is Cristiano of himself? That's the question!"

"I'll tell you something, Edo," said David. "When he was leaving at the end of last year, he said he was conscious of getting old. He more or less said that nobody is the same as they used to be. *Day by day, we are getting old—all of us. But you've got to adopt and know what your strengths are*, he said."[79]

"Yeah," said Edo. "But it was apparent that his perception of his own strengths was not the same as Erik ten Hag's idea of Cristiano's strengths. Cristiano still believed he was the best in the world. And recently, he got in trouble with the fans in Saudi Arabia when he grabbed his balls after they were chanting *Messi, Messi* to provoke him. He still can't accept certain things. Strangely, but significantly enough, he didn't even win the Saudi league with his Al-Nassr."

"Yeah," said David. "He's been struggling for the last year or so. But I must admit I'm happy he's struggling in Saudi Arabia rather than at Man United. We flourished after he left. After that disastrous start to the season, it seemed our club was about to fall apart. With Ronaldo on the bench and everything that went on before the World Cup, nobody could have predicted we would end the season in third place, win the League Cup and give Man City a fair contest in the FA Cup final."

"I see," said Edo.

"We stood up tall!" David chanted. "*Still proud to be Man United!*"

"Jeez, keep your voice down, David, would you? Remember where you are."

David grinned.

"Yeah, I forgot," he said. "Anyway, Ronaldo said that he thinks nobody in the game can adapt with age like he can. He's well aware he's not that fast-dribbling, ankle-breaking winger he was twenty years ago. So now he's almost forty and adopting a new style of play in Saudi Arabia."

"Cristiano changes to survive, yes," said Edo. "But I'm not sure how ready he is to change in his essence."

"I suppose," said David.

"He's not the same player as he was when he was twenty. He got that right," said Edo.

"Very true," said David. "When Ronaldo first came to Manchester, he was a trickster. His ball skills were on a different level—such profoundly powerful stepovers, nutmegs, backheels, rabonas, spins and turns. It was pure poetry. He moved like a ballet dancer, leaving his opponents baffled. He was quicker than others, and he saw more than them. His mind was sharp as a razor, and his legs were a channel for the pure creation he manifested. Opponents were in awe as they watched the eighteen-year-old who was dearly in love with the ball—just a kid who would seem as free as a bird when the ball came to him."

"Yeah, I guess he was drawing a bit of inspiration from the Ronaldinho source," said Edo. "Such beauty can't come from anywhere else."

"So when did the Ronaldinho in Ronaldo disappear?" said David.

Edo thought for a moment.

"The same place the Ronaldinho in all of us goes," said Edo. "It gets covered by the ego. The more Cristiano looked for status in his game, for meaning in his dribbling and creativity, the more his urge to become the best burst from his being, the more Ronaldinho state of consciousness was diminished. Although his love for the game has always been there, it has suffocated beneath the picture of a perfect man—*CR7*."

"Yes, but he was pressured to *change*!" barked David. "Ronaldo *must* have changed because even though he was a superstar already, there were doubts about him during his first three seasons in England. His game was *beautiful*, but to become great, he had to become more *effective*. At the beginning of the 2006 season—after the World Cup in Germany—a new man appeared in the United locker room—the new Ronaldo, the machine Ronaldo. He scored seventeen Premier League goals that season, becoming the central figure in the United team. Everything orbited around him after that."

"At the same time, he was less creative than before," said Edo.

"Yes, Edo," said David. "So you see—the laws of the game. Ego wins games. Creativity doesn't."

Edo and David looked deeply into each other's eyes as they approached Manchester Piccadilly station.

"Listen to me," said David. "Gary Neville—a man who grew up at the United academy and was taught to put the collective values of Man United above everything—said Ronaldo had taught him that it was possible to accommodate individual ambition within the team's aims and make them work together."[80]

"Wow," said Edo, gently clapping his hands.

"That's not all," said David. "Ronaldo also used to say, T*oo much water kills the plant,* to Gary Neville back then."

"Too much water kills the plant," Edo muttered, bowing his head. "He *did* know balance. He had some moments of pure wisdom, it would seem."

"A few years later," said David. "Real Madrid came for Ronaldo, and he adopted well again with his age. He became more muscular, so naturally, he could no longer be the winger who received the ball in his half. His new position was closer to the opponent's box. And by the time Ronaldo moved to Madrid, he was already a ruthless killer, a goal-scoring machine—not much of that pure trickster left."

"Yeah, that's when the records became his obsession," said Edo. "He focused on breaking one after another—doing everything to get in a position to score and screaming at his players when they didn't pass him the ball. The freedom of his mind was gone."

"All in the name of CR7," said David.

"All in the name of trauma, perhaps," said Edo. "Even though he had brief moments of Ronaldinho consciousness, there was a growing need to prove he deserved to live. Cristiano's will to be the best became stronger than his love for the game."

"Still," said David. "Only a few days ago, after his first season in Saudi Arabia, he said he learns the most when he is down and that it's a good thing that problems appear at certain moments. *When you are at the top of the wave, you don't see what is happening underneath.*[81] The image of *CR7*, the ultimate winner, can't coexist with the wisdom that accepts losses as part of the process, which makes me think that he's indeed changing in his essence as well."

"There you go," said Edo as the pair entered the train station.

"When you are on top, enjoy it while you can," said David. "And when you are at the bottom, *learn.*"

Edo nodded, placing a hand on his friend's shoulder.

The City fans filled the concourse, singing loudly. Their songs echoed around the platform, bouncing off porcelain walls and amplifying.

"In Madrid, as the seasons passed, the idea of CR7 became too big," said Edo.

"Yes, but with that rise also came four Champions League titles," said David. "Ronaldo's Real Madrid was *the* most dominant European force, winning title after title. He pushed his teammates to the edge, sowing that *never good enough* mentality in each of them."

"Absolutely," said Edo.

"And hence, the individual prizes came as well—the ones he values the most," said David. "*Four* Ballon d'Ors in his last six years in Madrid, finally equalling Messi's record of five *best-player in the world* awards."

"Yes," said Edo. "But later, Messi won two more, not including another probable one this year to close the investigation once and for all."

Edo pretended to dust his hands off while David sighed.

"At one point in Real Madrid," said David. "Even the Champions League trophies weren't enough for Ronaldo. He needed more trophies, new records to break, and new environments to dominate. That's why he went to Italy."

"Yeah, Juventus," said Edo. "And the story of how he ended up there is fascinating. The deal was sealed after that game Real Madrid played in Turin."

David looked deeply at his friend, who started miming football actions on the platform.

"Juventus were suffering 1-0 down. Carvajal crossed the ball in the box, seemingly wasting the opportunity," Edo said. "It looked like an easy job for the rock-solid Juventus defence. But—" Edo lifted his finger. "Out of nowhere, Cristiano ran towards the ball, turning his back to the great Gianluigi Buffon and jumping like a god. At that moment, the Juventus defenders realised what was about to happen, and that some acts of art simply can't be defended. Cristiano's foot kissed the ball perfectly in what was the most spectacular bicycle kick ever seen on a football pitch."

David had a tear in his eye as they passed the still-raging Manchester City fans.

"Cristiano stood up and ran towards the crowd," Edo continued. "And he was pointing to himself with his index finger as if to say, *I am number one*."

David listened in anticipation.

"But then something incredible happened," Edo said. "As he approached the Juventus fans, they applauded him, putting aside their role as opposition fans for a timeless moment, to hail Cristiano's universal art."

"There was only one club for Ronaldo after that," David said with a look of relief in his eyes.

"As he stood before those Juventus fans, the scene changed immediately," Edo said as the train home arrived. "And Cristiano's face changed permanently. That body posture of self-idolisation was gone, and he seemed humble for the first time—grateful even. He put his hand on his heart and thanked the fans. And among the misery and euphoria of that mad football match in Turin, Cristiano smiled a genuine smile—for a fleeting moment, his inner Ronaldinho shone like the sun and he looked like a child again."

A Message From the Author

Hi there!

This book has been quite a journey. Thank you for reading it!

If you liked it, why don't you spread the word? Tell your neighbour—a friend. Or just share a few words about it on social media.

If you go for the option of Instagram, don't forget to take a selfie of yourself holding the book—it will look more genuine. Just kidding, you don't need to do that!

Here are my social media accounts in case you want to connect.

Instagram: karlo_tasler

LinkedIn: karlo-tasler

Medium: @karlo-tasler

Thanks,

Karlo Tasler

Bibliography

The following sources correspond to the number markers in the text.

1. Sousa, Paulo, and Aveiro, Dolores, *Mae Coragem*, Materia Prima, 2014

2. Wonke, Martin, Gay-Rees and Kapadia, *Ronaldo* (documentary), NBC Universal, 2015

3. Ronaldo, Cristiano, 'Madrid: My story', *The Players' Tribune*, 2 October 2017

4. Ferguson, Ruhemann, *Sir Alex Ferguson never give in* (documentary), DNA Films and Passion Pictures, 2021

5. Pearce, James, 'Liverpool', *Liverpool Echo*, 9 April 2018

6. Klopp, Jurgen, 'Maybe I am dreaming', *The Players' Tribune,* 24 September 2019

7. 'New Liverpool manager Jurgen Klopp', *Youtube*, uploaded by On Demand News, 9 October 2015

8. Pearce, James and Huges, Simon, 'Jurgen Klopp—The fist-pumping genius', *The Athletic*, 26 June 2020

9. McMath, Hunter, Guillen, *Take the ball, pass the ball* (documentary), Zoom Sport International, 2018

10. Bjelogrlic, Petrovic, *Montevideo, Bog te video* (TV series), Intermedia Network, 2012-2014

11. Cvetkovic, Ivan, 'Nisam hteo da igram u drugom poluvremenu', *Politika,* 28 July 2020

12. Crafton, Adam, 'Herrera', *The Athletic*, 8 June 2020

13. 'Mourinho's legendary moment: I am a Special One', *Youtube,* uploaded by Football Daily, 4 June 2013

14. 'Jose Mourinho's first full press conference', *Youtube,* uploaded by TNT Sports, 21 November 2019

15. 'Jose Mourinho Presentation', *Youtube,* uploaded by Shivdes1, 31 May 2010

16. Ibrahimovic, Zlatan with Lagercrantz, David, *I Am Zlatan Ibrahimovic*, Penguin Books, 2011

17. 'Ciro Blazevic—Trening NK Zagreb', *Youtube,* uploaded by Casual29, 13 November 2012

18. 'Davor Suker's chip at EURO 96: Croatia v Denmark', *Youtube,* uploaded by UEFA, 9 November 2015

19. Fifield, Dominic, 'Ronaldinho', *The Guardian, 29 November 2005*

20. O'Rourke, Peter, 'Ronnie rules out English move', *Sky Sports*

21. 'Francesco Totti—The full farewell speech', *Youtube,* uploaded by AS Roma, 5 June 2017

22. O'Brien, Sean, 'Ronaldinho', *Talksport,* 14 March 2020

23. Adit, John, *Ronaldinho* (Prezi slideshow presentation), 10 December 2020

24. Barilla, Carmelo, 'Allegri', *Calcioweb,* 19 December 2019

25. Ronaldinho, 'Letter to my younger self', *The Players' Tribune,* 12 January 2017

26. Digby, Adam, 'Remembering Ronaldinho's excessive Milan nights', *Bleacher Report,* 14 July 2017

27. Segura, Arnau, 'Perfectamente sencillo, sencillamente perfecto', *Panenka,* 13 September 2018

28. 'Rio Ferdinand's between the lines', *Youtube,* uploaded by TNT Sports, 4 December 2020

29. Mork, Martin, 'Zlatan: Sent Materazzi to hospital', *Football Italia, 5 December 2019*

30. Stanley, Anton, 'Trashed', *Talksport,* 12 September 2018

31. Ferguson, Alex, *Alex Ferguson My Autobiography,* Hodder & Stoughton, 2013

32. 'Ibrahimovic's dressing room speech', *Youtube,* uploaded by AC Milan, 23 May 2022

33. 'Zlatan Ibrahimovic in Dubai: A special interview', *Youtube,* uploaded by AC Milan, 12 December 2022

34. 'Zlatan Ibrahimovic—I am football | The movie', *Youtube,* uploaded by Kannan Vaidyanath, 1 July 2020

35. Lyttleton, Ben, *Twelve Yards,* Corgi, 2014

36. Marland, Daniel, 'Julio Cesar', *Sportbible,* 12 February 2021

37. 'Mourinho tells funny Balotelli story', *Youtube,* uploaded by CNN, 19 August 2014

38. Bandini, Nicky, 'What made Liverpool's Mario Balotelli', *The Guardian*, 29 August 2014

39. 'Erik ten Hag full post-match press conference', *Youtube,* uploaded by Reddevilslatest, 2 October 2022

40. Gray, Ashley, 'Eduardo', *Daily Mail Online,* 29 November 2011

41. 'Eduardo's first TV interview after his injury', *Youtube,* uploaded by Mathmos, 5 March 2008

42. Tolic, Josip, 'Prosinecki popustio: Prvi put pozvao Hajrovica u zmajeve', *24sata*, 23 September 2019

43. 'This is our Champions League', *Youtube,* uploaded by TNT Sports, 6 May 2022

44. Thomas, Josh, 'Messi didn't need anything from me at Barcelona—Ronaldinho', *Goal,* 17 January 2020

45. De la Iglesia, Roures, *Messi* (documentary), Under the Milky Way, 2015

46. Mukherjee, Soham, 'It could be today', *Goal,* 17 January 2023

47. 'Man City documentary series 2021/22', *Youtube,* uploaded by Man City, 15 December 2022

48. Burton, Chris, 'Messi', *Goal,* 29 June 2019

49. 'Pep Guardiola: Mourinho es el puto jefe', *Youtube,* uploaded by Fulbito y Fullvaso, 27 April 2011

50. 'Jose Mourinho's angry reaction', *Youtube,* uploaded by The Telegraph, 28 April 2011

Jones, Mark, 'Xabi Alonso', *The Mirror,* 13 December 2017

2. Hynter, David, 'Champions', *The Guardian,* 19 April 2021

53. 'Fearless Foxes: Our Story', *Youtube,* uploaded by Leicester City, 2 April 2020

54. Parashar, Arthur, 'A player who scores', *Daily Mail Online,* 8 December 2022

55. 'Rio Ferdinand's between the lines', *Youtube,* uploaded by Rio Ferdinand Presents Five, 10 December 2020

56. Lambourne, Jack, 'Friends', *Talksport,* 17 December 2022

57. 'Ronaldinho: Messi helping Neymar like I helped him', *Fourfourtwo,* 17 July 2016

58. Rodrigues, James, Carter, *Neymar: The perfect chaos* (documentary series), Campfire, Makemake, 2022

59. 'I couldn't be in a better place', *Youtube,* uploaded by Man City, 23 November 2022

60. Austin, Simon, 'Guardiola', *Training Ground Guru,* 25 October 2018

61. Huerga, Elias, Johnstone, Fernandez, *All or nothing Manchester City* (documentary), Amazon Studios, 2018

62. Hilsum, James, 'One thing I regret', *TNT Sports,* 02 December 2022

63. 'Sometime I need to be less stubborn', *Youtube,* uploaded by ITV Sport, 6 August 2021

64. 'Press conference: Jack Grealish', *Youtube,* uploaded by Tottenham Fan Chris Cowlin, 21 September 2022

65. 'I trust Grealish unconditionally', *Youtube,* uploaded by Beanymansports, 17 September 2022

66. 'I don't care about skills', *Youtube, uploaded by Sky Sports Premier League,* 21 August 2022

67. 'My favourite player was Zlatan', *Youtube,* uploaded by Amazon Prime Video Sport, 11 March 2023

68. Brookes, Sam, 'Erling Haaland', *Daily Mail Online,* 15 September 2022

69. 'We need him more', *Youtube, uploaded by* Talking City—A Manchester City Podcast, 13 March 2023

70. 'Haaland similar to Messi except he's always happy', *Youtube,* uploaded by HaytersTV, 8 April 2023

71. 'You are a special player', *Youtube,* uploaded by Sky Sports Premier League, 22 May 2023

72. Perarnau, Marti, *Pep Guardiola The Evolution,* Arena Sport, 2016

73. 'Stunned Pep Guardiola', *Youtube,* uploaded by TNT Sports, 4 May 2022

74. 'We will have dinner together someday', *Youtube,* uploaded by Sky Sports Premier League, 10 April 2022

75. 'Pep Guardiola: Roberto De Zerbi', *Youtube,* uploaded by Sky Sports News, 23 May 2023

76. 'Manchester City treble winning trophy parade', *Youtube,* uploaded by Beanymansports, 12 June 2023

77. 'Jose Mourinho questions referee', *Youtube,* uploaded by Guardian Football, 1 June 2023

78. 'Inter Miami over FC Barcelona', *Youtube,* uploaded by Magicalmessi, 10 June 2023

79. 'The full Cristiano Ronaldo', *Youtube,* uploaded by Piers Morgan Uncensored, 18 November 2022

80. Guillem, Balague, *Cristiano Ronaldo The Biography,* W&N, 2015

81. 'Ask Cristiano Ronaldo anything', *Youtube,* uploaded by Binance, 7 June 2023

Printed in Great Britain
by Amazon

35881204R00153